OPPOSING VIEWPOINTS® SERIES

The North and South Poles

Other Books of Related Interest:

Opposing Viewpoints Series

The Environment

At Issue Series

Adaptation and Climate Change

Current Controversies Series

Global Warming

"Congress shall make
no law . . . abridging
the freedom of speech,
or of the press."

First Amendment to the U.S. Constitution

The basic foundation of our democracy is the First Amendment guarantee of freedom of expression. The Opposing Viewpoints Series is dedicated to the concept of this basic freedom and the idea that it is more important to practice it than to enshrine it.

OPPOSING
VIEWPOINTS®
SERIES

The North
and South Poles

Diane Andrews Henningfeld, Book Editor

GREENHAVEN PRESS
A part of Gale, Cengage Learning

GALE
CENGAGE Learning™

Detroit • New York • San Francisco • New Haven, Conn • Waterville, Maine • London

Christine Nasso, *Publisher*
Elizabeth Des Chenes, *Managing Editor*

© 2010 Greenhaven Press, a part of Gale, Cengage Learning.

Gale and Greenhaven Press are registered trademarks used herein under license.

For more information, contact:
Greenhaven Press
27500 Drake Rd.
Farmington Hills, MI 48331-3535
Or you can visit our Internet site at gale.cengage.com

For product information and technology assistance, contact us at

Gale Customer Support, 1-800-877-4253
For permission to use material from this text or product, submit all requests online at www.cengage.com/permissions

Further permissions questions can be emailed to permissionrequest@cengage.com

Articles in Greenhaven Press anthologies are often edited for length to meet page requirements. In addition, original titles of these works are changed to clearly present the main thesis and to explicitly indicate the author's opinion. Every effort is made to ensure that Greenhaven Press accurately reflects the original intent of the authors. Every effort has been made to trace the owners of copyrighted material.

Cover Image copyright © Michaeljor/Dreamstime.com and © Rcaucino/Dreamstime.com.

LIBRARY OF CONGRESS CATALOGING-IN-PUBLICATION DATA

The North and South poles / Diane Andrews Henningfeld, book editor.
    p. cm. -- (Opposing viewpoints)
    Includes bibliographical references and index.
    ISBN 978-0-7377-4534-4 (hardcover)
    ISBN 978-0-7377-4535-1 (pbk.)
    1. Polar regions--Juvenile literature. I. Henningfeld, Diane Andrews.
    G587.N63 2009
    910.911--dc22
                                                 2009018935

Printed in the United States of America
1 2 3 4 5 6 7 13 12 11 10 09

Contents

Why Consider Opposing Viewpoints?   11

Introduction   14

Chapter 1: Who Should Govern the North and South Poles?

Chapter Preface   19

1. Territorial Claims Threaten the Antarctic   22
   James Bone

2. The Antarctic Treaty System Provides   29
   the Best Governance
   British Antarctic Survey

3. Antarctica Should Be Governed by   38
   the United Nations
   Martin Lishexian Lee

4. Antarctica Should Be Governed Jointly by the   45
   United Nations and the Antarctic Treaty System
   Janet Belkin

5. Territorial Claims Threaten the Arctic   56
   Adam Wolfe

6. An Arctic Treaty Should Be Established   63
   Rasmus Ole Rasmussen

7. Canada Has Legal Claims to Arctic Territory   70
   and Waters
   François Côté and Robert Dufresne

8. The United States, Canada, and Denmark   80
   Should Jointly Control Arctic Waters
   Dianne DeMille

Periodical Bibliography   85

Chapter 2: How Does Climate Change Affect the North and South Poles?

Chapter Preface   87

1. The Polar Ice Melt Will Cause Ocean Levels   89
   to Rise Rapidly
   Colin Woodard

2. The Polar Ice Melt Will Not Cause Ocean   94
   Levels to Rise Rapidly
   Jerome J. Schmitt

3. Polar Indigenous Peoples Are Threatened   101
   by Climate Change
   Timo Koiurova, Henna Tervo, and Adam Stepien

4. Polar Indigenous Peoples Have Adapted   107
   to Climate Change in the Past
   Mirjam Macchi

5. Polar Bears Are Endangered by Climate Change   113
   Jamie Rappaport Clark

6. Polar Bears Are Not Endangered By   121
   Climate Change
   H. Sterling Burnett

Periodical Bibliography   127

Chapter 3: Should the Natural Resources of the Polar Regions Be Developed?

Chapter Preface   129

1. The Natural Resources of the Arctic Should   132
   Be Protected
   Falk Huettmann and Sue Hazlett

2. National Security Requires U.S. Development   137
   of the Arctic
   Ariel Cohen, Lajos F. Szaszdi and Jim Dolbow

3. Polar Indigenous Peoples May Benefit   143
   from Resource Development
   Felix von Geyer and Simon Handelsman

4. Polar Indigenous Peoples Will Be Harmed   149
   by Resource Development
   Macdonald Stainsby

5. The United States Must Drill for Oil   157
   in the Arctic
   Paul Driessen

6. The United States Should Not Drill   162
   for Oil in the Arctic
   Natural Resources Defense Council

Periodical Bibliography   168

Chapter 4: What Role Should Tourism Play in the North and South Poles?

Chapter Preface   170

1. Tourism Must Be Better Regulated in Antarctica   173
   The Antarctic and Southern Ocean Coalition

2. Tourism Is Well-Regulated in Antarctica   178
   Rebecca Roper-Gee

3. The Number of Tourists to Antarctica   185
   Should Be Limited
   Juan Kratzmaier

4. Polar Tourism Should Not Be Limited   191
   Simon Jenkins

Periodical Bibliography   197

For Further Discussion   198

Organizations to Contact   201

Bibliography of Books   207

Index   212

Why Consider Opposing Viewpoints?

> *"The only way in which a human being can make some approach to knowing the whole of a subject is by hearing what can be said about it by persons of every variety of opinion and studying all modes in which it can be looked at by every character of mind. No wise man ever acquired his wisdom in any mode but this."*
>
> *John Stuart Mill*

In our media-intensive culture it is not difficult to find differing opinions. Thousands of newspapers and magazines and dozens of radio and television talk shows resound with differing points of view. The difficulty lies in deciding which opinion to agree with and which "experts" seem the most credible. The more inundated we become with differing opinions and claims, the more essential it is to hone critical reading and thinking skills to evaluate these ideas. Opposing Viewpoints books address this problem directly by presenting stimulating debates that can be used to enhance and teach these skills. The varied opinions contained in each book examine many different aspects of a single issue. While examining these conveniently edited opposing views, readers can develop critical thinking skills such as the ability to compare and contrast authors' credibility, facts, argumentation styles, use of persuasive techniques, and other stylistic tools. In short, the Opposing Viewpoints Series is an ideal way to attain the higher-level thinking and reading skills so essential in a culture of diverse and contradictory opinions.

In addition to providing a tool for critical thinking, Opposing Viewpoints books challenge readers to question their own strongly held opinions and assumptions. Most people form their opinions on the basis of upbringing, peer pressure, and personal, cultural, or professional bias. By reading carefully balanced opposing views, readers must directly confront new ideas as well as the opinions of those with whom they disagree. This is not to simplistically argue that everyone who reads opposing views will—or should—change his or her opinion. Instead, the series enhances readers' understanding of their own views by encouraging confrontation with opposing ideas. Careful examination of others' views can lead to the readers' understanding of the logical inconsistencies in their own opinions, perspective on why they hold an opinion, and the consideration of the possibility that their opinion requires further evaluation.

Evaluating Other Opinions

To ensure that this type of examination occurs, Opposing Viewpoints books present all types of opinions. Prominent spokespeople on different sides of each issue as well as well-known professionals from many disciplines challenge the reader. An additional goal of the series is to provide a forum for other, less known, or even unpopular viewpoints. The opinion of an ordinary person who has had to make the decision to cut off life support from a terminally ill relative, for example, may be just as valuable and provide just as much insight as a medical ethicist's professional opinion. The editors have two additional purposes in including these less known views. One, the editors encourage readers to respect others' opinions—even when not enhanced by professional credibility. It is only by reading or listening to and objectively evaluating others' ideas that one can determine whether they are worthy of consideration. Two, the inclusion of such viewpoints encourages the important critical thinking skill of objectively evaluating an author's credentials and bias. This evaluation will illuminate an author's reasons for taking a particular stance on an issue and will aid in readers' evaluation of the author's ideas.

It is our hope that these books will give readers a deeper understanding of the issues debated and an appreciation of the complexity of even seemingly simple issues when good and honest people disagree. This awareness is particularly important in a democratic society such as ours in which people enter into public debate to determine the common good. Those with whom one disagrees should not be regarded as enemies but rather as people whose views deserve careful examination and may shed light on one's own.

Thomas Jefferson once said that "difference of opinion leads to inquiry, and inquiry to truth." Jefferson, a broadly educated man, argued that "if a nation expects to be ignorant and free . . . it expects what never was and never will be." As individuals and as a nation, it is imperative that we consider the opinions of others and examine them with skill and discernment. The Opposing Viewpoints Series is intended to help readers achieve this goal.

David L. Bender and Bruno Leone,
Founders

Introduction

The far north and the far south have long evoked a sense of wonder and awe. The frigid temperatures, the frozen landscape, and the howling winds all combine to make the polar regions the last frontiers on Earth for human exploration. The drive to be the first person to stand on the spot where all points are south, or all points are north, compelled twentieth century explorers to risk their lives, and the lives of their companions, to get there first.

However, long before the twentieth century, human beings traveled to the polar regions. Anthropologists believe Inuit people first arrived in the Arctic from Asia as many as 18,000 years ago, and they made their home in the ice and snow of the far north. Evidence also exists that Norse people traveled the icy waters in the years between 800 and 1000 CE. During the great age of European exploration, the Englishman John Cabot tried to find a quicker route to Asia through what he called the Northwest Passage. Indeed, many explorers set off from European shores in search of the riches of Asia only to perish in the far north.

In recognition of these early explorers, many of the waterways and islands of the Arctic bear their names: Hudson Bay, Baffin Island, and the Bering Strait. Although the indigenous peoples of the Arctic had their own names for these locations, Europeans were the first to transcribe them in writing, and so in many cases have continued to name these places. The North Pole, however, continued to elude explorers until the twentieth century.

To be clear, there is more than one North Pole, and it does not always stay in the same location; as Barry Lopez explains in his 1986 book, *Arctic Dreams*:

> The precise location of the most exact of these northern poles, the North Pole itself, varies. ... If the North Pole were a scribing stylus, I would trace a line every 428 days in the shape of an irregular circle, with a diameter varying from 25 to 30 feet. Over the years, these irregular circles would all fall within an area some 65 feet across, called the Chandler Circle. The average position of the center of this circle is the Geographic North Pole.

One of the most famous of the nineteenth century expeditions to the far north was that of Sir John Franklin, who mapped more than 3,000 miles of northern Canada, according to the British National Maritime Museum. In all, Franklin traveled four times to the Arctic. His last expedition, which included two boats and 129 men, left from England on May 19, 1845. None of the men was ever seen again. The mystery of Franklin's disappearance sparked some 39 rescue attempts, including one by the American Elisha Kent Kane, who spent 21 months with his boat trapped in ice before finally traveling about 800 miles on foot back to Greenland. According to Charles Cowing of the Elisha Kent Historical Society, only through the help of Inuit people did Kane and any of his men survive the long winters of their entrapment on the ice.

On March 1, 1909, Commander Robert E. Peary of the U.S. Navy, accompanied by Matthew A. Henson, an African

American Navy engineer and long time companion, began his long trek to the North Pole from Ellesmere Island, part of a Canadian territory. Although Peary had made many journeys to the Arctic, the North Pole always had been just out of his reach. His perseverance paid off: on April 6, 1909, along with Henson, and four Polar Inuit explorers, Peary claimed to have reached the North Pole.

The claim that the team was the first to reach the Pole was tainted, however, by a claim by Frederick A. Cook that he had reached the Pole a year before Peary. The controversy about who was the first, continues to this day, although Cook has been largely discredited in the intervening years. It is still unknown whether Peary actually reached the Pole, however.

Controversy also swirled around attempts to reach the South Pole. Ironically, Norwegian explorer Roald Amundsen had long wanted to reach the North Pole, and in 1905 he was the first person to navigate the Northwest Passage successfully. The controversy stirred up by Cook and Peary, however, turned his eyes southward. Amundsen set sail for Antarctica in June 1910. At the same time, the Englishman Robert Falcon Scott also was mounting an expedition for the South Pole. This was not Scott's first trip; he participated in the 1901–1904 expedition with Ernest Shackleton and Edward Wilson that came within 410 miles of achieving the Pole, according to Sian Flynn in "The Race to the South Pole," for the British Broadcasting Corporation.

In 1911, both Scott and Amundsen began their journeys. According to Flynn, they organized their expeditions in very different ways. Amundsen was extremely detail oriented and kept a single-minded focus on his goal of reaching the South Pole. Although they shared the same ultimate goal, Scott conducted scientific studies along the way. For Scott, the honor of England was at stake. Norway, on the other hand, was a young nation, having just won its independence in 1905, as Flynn notes.

Overall, Amundsen's expedition was better prepared for the elements. They had warmer clothing, traversed much of the ground on skis, used dog sleds for one way, and then used the dogs for food on the way back. As a result, the Norwegians reached the Pole on December 15, 1911. Scott, on the other hand, encountered difficulties nearly every step of the way. After a grueling trip, he and his team finally reached the South Pole, only to discover that Amundsen had been there a month before him.

On the return trip, Scott and his men encountered more trouble. Ultimately, Scott and his four companions perished. Their remains, along with Scott's journals, were recovered eight months later. Scott became a national hero in Britain, and his loss was greatly mourned.

The stories of the great Arctic and Antarctic explorers provide a context for the viewpoints that follow. The extreme climate and conditions of the polar regions open many questions, addressed in the following chapters: Who Should Govern the North and South Poles?; How Does Climate Change Affect the North and South Poles?; Should the Natural Resources of the Polar Regions Be Developed?; and What Role Should Tourism Play in the North and South Poles? The writers of the viewpoints examine these questions from a variety of perspectives.

OPPOSING VIEWPOINTS® SERIES

Who Should Govern the North and South Poles?

Chapter Preface

One question that frequently surfaces as people begin to study the Arctic and the Antarctic is this: "Who owns the North and South Poles?" The answer is not as simple as one might imagine. Antarctica is governed by the Antarctic Treaty System, signed by a group of nations that agree that Antarctica should be a place for science and research and that no one nation owns the continent. However, because Antarctica was uninhabited before its initial exploration by Europeans, Americans, and Asians, there are no indigenous peoples to factor into its governance.

Such is not the case with the Arctic. More than four million indigenous peoples, belonging to forty or more groups, live in the far north, in territories claimed by the United States, Canada, Russia, Denmark (through Greenland and the Faroe Islands), Norway, Sweden, and Finland. (Although Iceland is an Arctic country, there are no indigenous minorities living there; Iceland's population is descended almost entirely from Scandinavian and Celtic settlers.) In Alaska, the indigenous peoples are members of the Iñupiaq, Yup'ik Inuit, Alutiq (sometimes called Aleuts), and Athabaskan groups. In Canada and Greenland, most indigenous peoples are Inuit. The Chukchi and Nenets live in northern Siberia, and the Sámi live across the northern portions of Norway, Sweden, and Finland. There are many other smaller groups of indigenous peoples in the region.

In the past, when the Arctic regions were largely inaccessible and natural resources nearly impossible to mine, the indigenous peoples of the north were able to continue their traditional forms of life, with little governmental interference. During the twentieth and twenty-first centuries, however, the discovery of valuable minerals and oil has made the territories on which the indigenous peoples reside increasingly valuable to those nations that claim Arctic territory.

According to Jessica Shadian in her article, "Searching for the Indigenous Voice in a New Arctic Scramble: Berlin Conference Part II or a New Global Politics," "Historically, the Arctic has held a definitive place in global politics. This history, however, is one defined and written about far from the Arctic itself." In other words, those nations with territorial claims in the Arctic have not consulted with the peoples who live there in constructing a history of the place.

With the melting of Arctic sea ice, it is likely that the Northwest Passage will become open again. The Northwest Passage is an important political, economic, and strategic territory for the nation that controls it. At present, Canada asserts that the waters of the Northwest Passage are internal Canadian waterways. In addition, in 2007, Russia planted a flag on the ocean floor to assert its claim to the polar region. In the United States, high gasoline prices in 2008 led leaders to look north to Alaska for potential drilling.

In the rush to exploit the natural resources and strategic location of the Arctic, European and North American nations must now contend with the indigenous peoples who have organized themselves in groups such as the Aleut International Association, the Inuit Circumpolar Council, the Athabaskan Association and the Sámi Parliament, among many others. These groups are represented in the Arctic Council, which also has representatives from the eight Arctic member states. It remains to be seen how effective the Arctic Council will be in protecting the rights and the environment of the Arctic indigenous peoples. As Shadian asks, "Will the Arctic players set the rules together, or once again be on the sidelines of history while the future political and [economic] well-being is decided for them?"

The writers of the following viewpoints examine territorial claims of the Arctic region from many differing perspectives.

It is likely that the question of who owns the Arctic is one that will reverberate for many decades to come.

> *"Polar experts fear that rival national claims could lead to conflict as global warming makes it increasingly tempting to exploit mineral resources . . . in the Antarctic."*

Territorial Claims Threaten the Antarctic

James Bone

In the following viewpoint, James Bone argues that an increasing number of rival nations are staking claims in Antarctica. Because many of these claims overlap, he fears such claims will lead to conflict. In particular, Britain, Chile, and Argentina all claim portions of the Antarctic peninsula that eventually might be accessible for mineral exploitation, according to Bone, in spite of the provisions of the Antarctic Treaty System. Bone is a reporter for the British newspaper, The Times.

As you read, consider the following questions:

1. How much additional territory does Britain intend to claim in Antarctica, according to the viewpoint?

2. How much does it cost tourists for an overnight stay at the Chilean base in Antarctica, according to Bone?

3. In a move that Bone calls a "diplomatic coup," who did Chile host in Antarctica on November 9, 2007, and how could such a visit affect the politics of the region?

The children who live on Chile's Eduardo Frei Montalva Air Force Base are pawns in a great game in the Antarctic that they can but dimly understand.

The cluster of snowbound cabins, a 2½ hour flight from the tip of South America to the bottom of the world, is home to a permanent population of eighty that includes ten married couples with a total of 12 children, aged 1 to 17. Residents describe the remote outpost as a colonia.

"It's strange and difficult but it's super-beautiful," said Alumna Jofré, 12, whose father is chief of operations at the ice-covered airfield. "We have had amazingly beautiful experiences. We ski and snowboard and sledge."

There are downsides: "It's always the same. We go to the gym or to school. We always see the same people. It's a little complicated."

Overlapping Claims

Antarctica, once the torment of [British] explorers such as [Robert Falcon] Scott and [Ernest Henry] Shackleton, is slowly being settled by mankind as rival nations make overlapping claims to the vast expanse that is a tenth of the total landmass of the Earth. Global warming, shrinking ice and soaring oil prices all conspire to fuel competition for the world's final frontier. Britain has rattled its rivals by signalling that it intends effectively to extend its Antarctic territory by more than 50 per cent by claiming an additional 386,000 sq miles (100,000 sq km) of the adjoining seabed.

The Frei base sits on King George Island, off the tip of the Antarctic Peninsula on territory claimed by Britain and Argentina as well as Chile. Once a remote whaling station, the island is now known as the unofficial "capital of Antarctica".

The first surprise on landing in a Chilean military C130 transport aircraft is that my BlackBerry works. I check my e-mail and call my startled wife in New York to tell her that I am surrounded by luminous turquoise-tinted icebergs.

As well as its own mobile phone signal, the Frei base boasts a bank, a post office, a hospital, a supermarket, a bar, a chapel, a school and an FM radio station, provocatively called Sovereignty.

At Russia's nearby Bellingshausen base, staff have reconstructed a wooden Orthdox church with a decorative spire that was first built in Siberia. At the Great Wall base beyond that, the Chinese operate a gift shop selling penguin statuettes to tourists who come ashore from cruise ships.

A short flight over King George Island in a 12-seat Twin Otter ski-plane reveals not only majestic icebergs sculpted into extraordinary geometric forms and colonies of sea lions and penguins but also groups of corrugated-iron cabins and Anderson shelters that make up the international bases. Argentina, Brazil, Poland, South Korea and Uruguay all maintain year-round research stations near the Chilean, Russian and Chinese bases.

Preventing a new Falklands-style conflict [a war fought between the United Kingdom and Argentina over disputed Falkland Islands] is the fact that Britain, Argentina and Chile are all signatories to the 1959 Antarctic Treaty, which voluntarily freezes the overlapping sovereignty claims. Nevertheless, Chile treats the aircraft ride from the southern city of Punta Arenas on the South American mainland to the Frei base in Antarctica as an internal flight that does not require a passport.

A travel agency in Punta Arenas even offers flights for tourists at $2,500 (£1,200) for a day-trip and $3,500 for an-

One Continent, Many Claims

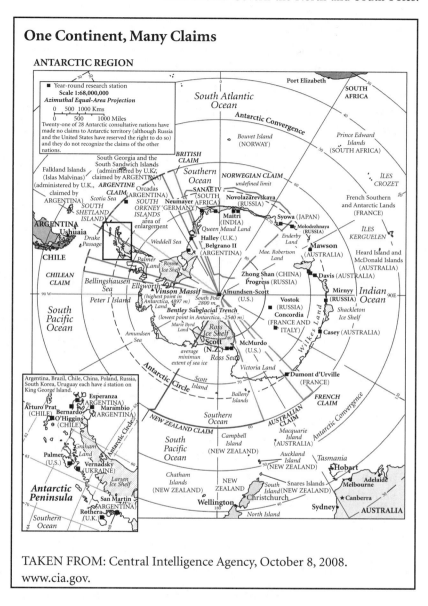

ANTARCTIC REGION

TAKEN FROM: Central Intelligence Agency, October 8, 2008.
www.cia.gov.

overnight stay at the Chilean base. Once they are there, Chilean soldiers will sell them a souvenir T-shirt emblazoned with a penguin and the words "Chilean Antarctica".

Establish Sovereignty

All three countries continue to affirm sovereignty by deliberately asserting their presence on the icy continent. Linda Capper, a spokeswoman for the British Antarctic Survey, which runs British research stations in the Antarctic, said that Britain performs administrative acts in the territory—a traditional test of sovereignty.

The British Antarctic Territory issues its own postage stamps and all British research stations have their own post office. British base commanders are sworn in as magistrates and conduct official duties such as stamping visitors' passports. But Britain is lagging in the "baby race" in Antarctica that its rivals Chile and Argentina seem bent on pursuing.

Argentina, intent on establishing sovereignty by having its citizens born in the disputed territory, resorted to flying Silvia Morella de Palma, the seven-months pregnant wife of an Argentine army captain, to the Esperanza base that her husband commanded. When she gave birth to Emilio Marcos de Palma on January 7, 1978, he became the first "native-born" Antarctican. Chile responded in kind when Juan Pablo Camacho was born at the Frei base to become the first Chilean born in Antarctica. Residents say that two more Chilean babies have since been born at Frei. No British baby has been born at a British Antarctic research station, Ms Capper said.

The 1991 Madrid Protocol to the Antarctic Treaty declares the icy continent "a natural reserve, devoted to peace and science" and outlaws mining or oil-drilling for 50 years.

Conflict Ahead

But polar experts fear that the rival national claims could lead to conflict as global warming makes it increasingly tempting to exploit mineral resources, such as oil and gas, in the Antarctic, particularly on the more accessible Antarctic Peninsula.

Gazing out over the unspoilt waters, Gino Casassa, a Chilean scientist and member of the Nobel Peace Prize-winning

Intergovernmental Panel on Climate Change, said that he is afraid that there will be oil platforms off King George Island in 50 years' time.

"This is a big threat," he said. "I would not like to see that happen but it will be inevitable. There will be a big fight over these competing issues: keeping it pristine for scientific work and the exploitation of resources. Especially with deglacierisation, it can become commercially viable."

Jack Child, the author of *Antarctica and South American Geopolitics*, said: "Looking ahead 20, 30, 40, 50 years, with new technologies and depletion of oil there might be an attempt to undermine the treaty to get at that oil."

He said that finding oil on the Antarctic Peninsula was "the worst possible scenario, but also the most possible".

Britain made diplomatic waves by confirming last month [October 2007] that it may soon file a claim to 386,000 square miles of seabed with the UN [United Nations], based on the continental shelf extending out from British Antarctic Territory. Chile and Argentina announced that they would lodge similar claims. Chile said that it would reopen its Arturo Prat naval base next year. And China dispatched 91 scientists yesterday to expand its two research stations and build a third station near Dome A, a forbidding inland plateau at an altitude of 4,000 metres (13,000 ft).

"Our big concern is that everyone says it's simply to file their claim, yet it's clear there is this domino response from the Antarctic claimants," said Karen Sack, head of oceans for the environmentalist group Greenpeace.

Chile scored a diplomatic coup on Friday [November 9, 2007] by hosting Ban Ki Moon, the UN Secretary-General, on a visit to Antarctica. Although the UN chief toured bases belonging to Chile, Uruguay and his native South Korea, he flew on board a Chilean military aircraft sitting beside the Chilean Environment Minister and UN Ambassador.

But Mr Ban, perhaps unwittingly, appeared to endorse an idea originally proposed by Malaysia and other developing nations in the late 1980s to declare Antarctica the "common heritage of mankind"—a proposal opposed by Antarctic claimants such as Britain, Argentina and Chile. Mr Ban declared: "This is a common heritage. We must preserve all this continent in an environmentally responsible way."

> *"The Antarctic Treaty System . . . has become recognised as one of the most successful sets of international agreements, setting an example of peaceful cooperation for the rest of the world."*

The Antarctic Treaty System Provides the Best Governance

British Antarctic Survey

According to the British Antarctic Survey, the Antarctic Treaty, signed in 1959 by twelve nation members remains a successful example of international cooperation in the governance of Antarctica. The authors assert that the Antarctic Treaty System (ATS) works closely with other organizations to protect and preserve the continent. The ATS, according to the authors, continues to demonstrate its commitment to disarmament and to preserving Antarctica for science. As such, the authors state, the treaty is one of the most successful international agreements ever developed. The British Antarctic Survey is an environmental research center and is responsible for British study of Antarctica.

As you read, consider the following questions:

1. Describe the first substantial multinational research program in Antarctica.

2. The ATS includes recommendations, measures, decisions, and resolutions of the Consultative Meetings relating to what matters?

3. What is the name of an industry body representing the interest of the growing tourist trade in Antarctica?

There are few places in the world where there has never been war, where the environment is fully protected, and where scientific research has priority. But there is a whole continent like this—it is the land the Antarctic Treaty parties call "... *a natural reserve, devoted to peace and science*".

At the southern end of our world, those who share the challenges of distance and cold to visit the ice-bound continent have developed a tradition of warm cooperation. Such cooperation, unique on this scale, is cemented by the Antarctic Treaty. . . .

A Land of Ice and Snow

The Antarctic continent is vast. It embraces the South Pole with permanent ice and snow. It is encircled by floating barriers of ice, stormy seas and appalling weather. Its great altitude chills the air to extremes, and its descent to sea level across a moving ice sheet generates the world's strongest winds. The cycling seasons reveal the spectacular natural forces of our planet. The surrounding seas teem with wildlife. And just 2% of this continent is free of ice, allowing a small toe-hold for hardy animals and plants.

The weather and isolation dominate all who visit. The discovery and exploration of Antarctica was shaped by the continent's remoteness and its extraordinarily inhospitable environment. These factors combined for centuries to keep humans away from all but the subantarctic islands and parts of the Southern Ocean where whaling and sealing took place. In human historic terms, the land exploration of Antarctica is recent, most of it being accomplished during the twentieth century.

The improved technology and knowledge of the last 100 years allowed greater access to the continent, encouraging detailed surveying and research, and the gradual occupation of Antarctica by scientific stations. By mid-[twentieth] century, permanent stations were being established and planning was underway for the International Geophysical Year (IGY) in 1957–58, the first substantial multi-nation research program in Antarctica. By mid-[twentieth] century, territorial positions had also been asserted, but not agreed, creating a tension that threatened future scientific cooperation.

The IGY was recognised as pivotal to the scientific understanding of Antarctica. The twelve nations active in Antarctica, nine of which made territorial claims or reserved the right to do so, agreed that their political and legal differences should not interfere with the research program. The outstanding success of the IGY led these nations to agree that peaceful scientific cooperation in the Antarctic should continue indefinitely. Negotiation of such an agreement, the Antarctic Treaty, commenced immediately after the IGY.

The Antarctic Treaty: A Model of Cooperation

The Antarctic Treaty was signed in Washington [D.C.] on 1 December 1959 by the twelve nations that had been active during the IGY (Argentina, Australia, Belgium, Chile, France, Japan, New Zealand, Norway, South Africa, United Kingdom, United States and USSR). The Treaty, which applies to the area south of 60° South latitude, is surprisingly short, but remarkably effective. Through this agreement, the countries active in Antarctica consult on the uses of a whole continent,

Members of the Antarctic Treaty System (ATS)

In addition to the twelve original member nations, the Treaty provides that any member state of the United Nations can join. Membership as of 2008 included the 12 original signatories, 16 additional consultative nations (those who conduct research in Antarctica and thus have voting rights) and 18 non-consultative members who attend the meetings but do not participate in decision making.

Country	First Membership Year	Status
Argentina	1961	Original signatory
Australia	1961	Original signatory
Austria	1987	Non-consultative
Belgium	1961	Original signatory
Belarus	2006	Non-consultative
Brazil	1975	Consultative
Bulgaria	1978	Consultative
Canada	1988	Non-consultative
Chile	1961	Original signatory
China	1985	Consultative
Colombia	1989	Non-consultative
Cuba	1984	Non-consultative
Czech Republic	1993	Non-consultative
Denmark	1965	Non-consultative
Ecuador	1987	Consultative
Estonia	2001	Non-consultative
Finland	1984	Consultative
France	1961	Original signatory
Germany	1979	Consultative
Guatemala	1991	Non-consultative
Hungary	1991	Non-consultative
India	1983	Consultative
Italy	1981	Consultative
Japan	1961	Original signatory
North Korea	1987	Non-consultative
South Korea	1976	Consultative

[CONTINUED]

[CONTINUED]

Members of the Antarctic Treaty System (ATS)

In addition to the twelve original member nations, the Treaty provides that any member state of the United Nations can join. Membership as of 2008 included the 12 original signatories, 16 additional consultative nations (those who conduct research in Antarctica and thus have voting rights) and 18 non-consultative members who attend the meetings but do not participate in decision making.

Country	First Membership Year	Status
Netherlands	1967	Consultative
New Zealand	1961	Original signatory
Norway	1961	Original signatory
Papua New Guinea	1975	Non-consultative
Peru	1981	Consultative
Poland	1961	Consultative
Romania	1971	Non-consultative
Russian Federation	1961	Original signatory
Slovak Republic	1993	Non-consultative
South Africa	1961	Original signatory
Spain	1982	Consultative
Sweden	1984	Consultative
Switzerland	1990	Non-consultative
Turkey	1996	Non-consultative
Ukraine	1992	Consultative
United Kingdom	1961	Original signatory
United States	1961	Original signatory
Uruguay	1980	Consultative
Venezuela	1999	Non-consultative

TAKEN FROM: Compiled by Editor.

with a commitment that it should not become the scene or object of international discord. In its fourteen articles the Treaty:

- stipulates that Antarctica should be used exclusively for peaceful purposes, military activities, such as the establishment of military bases or weapons testing, are specifically prohibited;

- guarantees continued freedom to conduct scientific research, as enjoyed during the IGY;

- promotes international scientific cooperation including the exchange of research plans and personnel, and requires that results of research be made freely available;

- sets aside the potential for sovereignty disputes between Treaty parties by providing that no activities will enhance or diminish previously asserted positions with respect to territorial claims, provides that no new or enlarged claims can be made, and makes rules relating to jurisdiction;

- prohibits nuclear explosions and the disposal of radioactive waste;

- provides for inspection by observers, designated by any party, of ships, stations and equipment in Antarctica to ensure the observance of, and compliance with, the Treaty;

- requires parties to give advance notice of their expeditions; provides for the parties to meet periodically to discuss measures to further the objectives of the Treaty; and

- puts in place a dispute settlement procedure and a mechanism by which the Treaty can be modified.

The Treaty also provides that any member of the United Nations can accede to it. The Treaty now [in 2008] has 46 signatories, 28 are Consultative Parties on the basis of being original signatories or by conducting substantial research there. Membership continues to grow.

A Record of Success

Since entering into force on 23 June 1961, the Treaty has been recognised as one of the most successful international agreements. Problematic differences over territorial claims have been effectively set aside and as a disarmament regime it has been outstandingly successful. The Treaty parties remain firmly committed to a system that is still effective in protecting their essential Antarctic interests. Science is proceeding unhindered.

Since the first Antarctic Treaty Consultative Meeting (ATCM) in 1961, the parties have met frequently, now annually, to discuss issues as diverse as scientific cooperation, measures to protect the environment, and operational issues—and they are committed to taking decisions by consensus. This process has allowed the Antarctic Treaty to evolve into a system with a number of components that meet the special needs of managing activities in the Antarctic, while protecting national interests. This regime is now known by the broader title of the Antarctic Treaty System, [ATS] which operates under the umbrella of the annual ATCM.

The Antarctic Treaty System comprises the Treaty itself and a number of related agreements. It also includes a range of organisations that contribute to the work of the decision-making forums.

In addition to the related agreements (described below), the Treaty System includes the recommendations, measures, decisions and resolutions of the Consultative Meetings relating to matters such as:

- scientific cooperation;

- protection of the Antarctic environment;

- conservation of plants and animals;

- preservation of historic sites;

- designation and management of protected areas;

- management of tourism;

- information exchange;

- collection of meteorological data;

- hydrographic charting;

- logistic cooperation; and

- communications and safety.

The Treaty parties have put in place rules relating to specific issues. The development of these agreements has allowed the implementation, with greater precision, of legally binding provisions for the regulation of activities in Antarctica.

Working Together: The Experts and the ATS

Apart from the legal instruments and measures outlined above, a number of specialised bodies assist the Treaty parties in the conduct of their work. Specific tasks may be directed to these bodies, or they may be invited to provide observers or experts to participate in Treaty forums.

The Scientific Committee on Antarctic Research (SCAR) coordinates Antarctic research programs and encourages scientific cooperation. Through its various subordinate groups it is able to provide expert information on a range of disciplines and on the scientific implications of operational proposals of the Treaty meetings.

The Council of Managers of National Antarctic Programs [COMNAP] comprises the heads of each of the national Antarctic operating agencies. COMNAP meets annually to exchange logistic information, encourage cooperation and develop advice to the Treaty parties on a range of practical matters.

The Antarctic Treaty parties have also developed a close relationship with environmental inter-governmental and non-government organisations that represent the broader community interests in conservation. Organisations such as the International Union for the Conservation of Nature, the United

Nations Environment Program and the Antarctic and Southern Ocean Coalition are also invited to the Treaty meetings as experts.

Bodies with technical expertise relevant to the Treaty discussions also participate. They include the International Hydrographic Organisation, the World Meteorological Organisation and the Intergovernmental Oceanographic Commission.

The International Association of Antarctic Tour Operators [IAATO] is an industry body representing the interests of the growing tourist trade in Antarctica. Many tour operators are affiliated with IAATO, which also provides experts to the annual Treaty meetings.

The Treaty provided that any party could call for a review conference after the expiration of 30 years. No party has done so. In 1991, on the thirtieth anniversary of the Treaty, the parties recognised the continuing strength and relevance of the Treaty by adopting a declaration recording their determination to maintain and strengthen the Treaty and to protect Antarctica's environmental and scientific values.

Under the Treaty, each party has enjoyed peaceful cooperation and freedom of scientific research. That research has contributed significantly to knowledge of the Earth and is contributing to the protection of the global environment. Environmental monitoring in Antarctica has, for example, led to the discovery of the seasonal depletion of atmospheric ozone over the Antarctic.

As the Antarctic Treaty System matures it has become recognised as one of the most successful sets of international agreements, setting an example of peaceful cooperation for the rest of the world.

As an environmental regime it is unique—an entire continent, which is essentially undisturbed, will remain protected because of the commitment and cooperation of the Treaty parties.

"*The administration of Antarctic affairs [should] be under a world government . . . [I]t would be . . . realistic to encourage the United Nations to evolve in this way.*"

Antarctica Should Be Governed by the United Nations

Martin Lishexian Lee

In the following viewpoint, Martin Lishexian Lee argues that although the Antarctic Treaty System (ATS) has successfully managed Antarctica for more than forty years, there are incurable defects in the approach, including the inability of the ATS to enforce its own terms. He further asserts that the ATS will be unable to meet the "growing needs to protect the Antarctic environment." Therefore, he argues, the United Nations must become a more centralized organization with the power to settle Antarctic territorial claims and enforce environmental restrictions. Lee is a lawyer who argues before the Supreme Court of Tasmania, Australia.

Martin Lishexian Lee, "A Case for World Government of the Antarctic," *Gonzaga Journal of International Law*, vol. 73, 2005, pp. 76–95. Reproduced by permission.

As you read, consider the following questions:

1. In what year was the Antarctic Treaty signed, and how did the era affect its formation, according to Lee?

2. What are two things the ATS has prevented in Antarctica, according to Lee?

3. What are some of the new challenges facing the ATS, according to Lee?

A pristine Antarctica is important to scientific research and stabilizing the planetary environment. However, in the late 1940's, conflict arose among the sovereign states claiming territory in Antarctica. There was potential militarization in the continent between two superpowers, the United States and the Soviet Union, both of which had significant interests there. Born in the Cold War times, the Antarctic Treaty itself sought to demilitarize Antarctica, promote freedom of scientific research and encourage international co-operation. Subsequently, in order to accommodate various needs and international circumstances, a mechanism has gradually evolved focusing on comprehensive environmental protection, the Antarctic Treaty System.

In the past forty years, the mechanism has successfully achieved its goals. As a vehicle of collective administration, the Antarctic Treaty System has preserved the continent, ensured freedom of scientific research, and circumvented territorial claim problems. The key to success is its unique freezing and bifocalism [two distinct goals] approach: seeking for non-solutions to sovereignty issues and leaving deep conflicts to future resolution. However, it is this approach, arguably, which contributes to the weak enforcement of the obligations. Uncertainty of territorial sovereignty leads to jurisdiction difficulties. This, in combination with the ambiguity and loopholes present in the instruments and recommendations of the regime, the hortatory [urging a course of action] nature of those recommendations, consensus and veto powers, self-policing policy, lack of third party effects, and other factors, hinders enforcement of compliance under the system.

Incurable Defects in the Antarctic Treaty System

These defects are perceived as incurable in the current structure due to the inherent problem of territorial conflict and the basic principle of consent in treaty law. While the regime has been successful in the past, it may not be able to cope with the challenges of the 21st century, which include floods of tourists, illegal fishing and scientific research, and potential mining interests and development. Therefore, the Antarctic Treaty System should further evolve to accommodate the new circumstances. . . .[T]he administration of Antarctic affairs [should] be under a world government. While the political reality indicates the difficulty of establishing a new world government, it would be more realistic to encourage the United Nations (UN) to evolve in this way. The fundamental features of this proposed system are that its administration is not based on consent and States must relinquish their external sovereignty. This author argues that this would eliminate the inherited defects of the current regime, enabling the Antarctic Treaty System to achieve further triumphs when facing the new challenges.

Background of the Antarctic Treaty System

Antarctica is one of the most vast, primarily unexplored areas, and the coldest, driest environment on earth. It is important to scientific research, and plays a significant role in stabilizing the planetary environment. In the late 1940s the conflict between nations claiming territory in the Antarctic region opened up. The potential for militarization of the continent existed between the United States and the Soviet Union, both of which had significant Antarctic interests. At the time, the potential existed for Antarctica to become a pawn in the Cold War. Born in such an era, the Antarctic Treaty, which was concluded in 1959, sought to deal with the major issues current then and itself made virtually no reference to the environment. It provides that Antarctica is to be used for peaceful purposes only and no military bases are to be established on the continent. Freedom of scientific research is encouraged with mechanisms to promote international cooperation. Subsequently, with the accommodation to new circumstances and needs, and changing priorities among the Consultative Parties [nations participating in the Antarctic Treaty System], the regime has evolved to a structure emphasizing environmental protection. Defined in the Antarctic Treaty, the Antarctic System governs the application of the measures in effect under the Treaty, its associated separate international instruments in force, and the measures in effect under those instruments. Currently, there are five separate instruments in force and one is legally dead.

The Antarctic Treaty System has managed Antarctica effectively to date. It has not only avoided conflicts over sovereignty and prevented the militarization of the continent, but also prevented an unregulated gold rush in Antarctica. As a "vehicle for collective administration," the system has attained "three landmark achievements," i.e. reservation of Antarctica, ensuring freedom of science, and removal of the territorial claim problem. . . .

Flexible Approach, Weak Enforcement

Nevertheless, it is this flexible approach which contributes to the weak enforcement. It is true that by seeking this flexible non-solution for sovereignty issues, the deepest conflict in relation to territorial claims may be temporarily put aside. However, merely maintaining the status quo will not ensure that it can respond to the growing needs to protect the Antarctic environment. . . .

New Rules Needed to Govern World's Fragile Polar Regions

A new co-ordinated international set of rules to govern commercial and research activities in both of Earth's polar regions is urgently needed to reflect new environmental realities and to temper pressure building on these highly fragile ecosystems, according to several of the experts convening in Iceland for a UN-affiliated conference marking the International Polar Year. . . .

Antarctica is witnessing a growing parade of tourists (40,000, including tour staff, in 2007), as well as researchers (now about 4,000 in summer occupying 37 permanent stations and numerous field camps) and companies interested in exploiting the biological properties of that continent's "extremophiles [organisms that thrive in physically or geochemically extreme conditions]."

"New Rules Needed to Govern World's Fragile Polar Regions,"
Science Daily, *September 8, 2008. www.sciencedaily.com.*

This article submits that a realistic solution is to encourage the UN to evolve into a vertical governmental institution. At this stage the UN already possesses some "elements of global [governance]." Along these lines, it may first evolve to a structure like the European Union, and then further to a more centralized institution, i.e. world government elected by world citizens. At that time, states are no longer the major players in the UN, and we would have a real global community. The process of economic globalization indicates this trend and likelihood, and is described as "an unstoppable force hurtling toward immovable object-state sovereignty." The Antarctic Treaty System, when it accommodates this trend, would become a part of this force.

Antarctica Under a World Government

Born in the age of the Cold War and shouldered with the task to promote peace, freedom of scientific research and international cooperation, the Antarctic Treaty System has successfully turned the potential militarization in the Antarctic continent into a peaceful reserve. During this process, the Antarctic Treaty System itself has also evolved to a comprehensive environmental protection regime. In achieving these triumphs, to freeze the different parties' legal position in relation to their territorial claims has been the key to success.

Nevertheless, it is the strategy to freeze the sovereignty issue which has substantially led to the weak enforcement of the regime. Uncertainty about the territorial sovereignty over Antarctica results in jurisdiction difficulties in the exercise of control over the activities in that region. There are a combination of other factors, such as ambiguity and loopholes in the instruments and recommendations, the self-policing policy, hortatory approach, consensus and veto powers, which mean that enforcement is weak.

Now the Antarctic Treaty System is facing new challenges for the new century. Increases in tourist numbers, illegal fishing and increased scientific research, and potential mining activities are becoming serious threats to the Antarctic environment. The current administrative structure of the Antarctic Treaty System would not be able to deal with these threats due to the above weaknesses. These defects are, arguably, incurable unless the sovereignty claims are relinquished and the consensual basis of the regime can be eliminated. Thus, it is unavoidable to re-organize the administration of the Antarctic Treaty System.

This author advocates that the Antarctic Treaty System should become a regime under a world government administration. Under such an administration, states are required to relinquish sovereignty. Differing from the UN, this government has vertical powers and has a mandatory executive model. It is compulsory for parties to appear in front of the ICJ [International Court of Justice] or other judicial bodies for legal proceedings and consensus will no longer be the prerequisite for their jurisdictions. Individuals should not be excluded on the grounds of lack of standing. Due to the political reality, it is practical to encourage the UN to evolve into a world government. The first stage may take the form of the European Union, and then move to be a more centralized institution. It is perceived that this administrative model would cure the inborn defects of sovereignty disputes and veto power, both of which hinder the effective administration and enforcement of the current Antarctic regime. In the light of the globalization process, this author believes that the Antarctic Treaty System, when it accommodates this trend and the new challenges, would add its own force to globalization, ringing the "funeral bells" for the "old notion of state sovereignty."

"*Involving an international organization in the governance of Antarctica- ...seems a more realistic way of keeping the [Antarctic Treaty System] in place and [more] effective than would permitting it to continue with no enforcement capability.*"

Antarctica Should Be Governed Jointly by the United Nations and the Antarctic Treaty System

Janet Belkin

In the following viewpoint, Janet Belkin argues that the Antarctic Treaty System (ATS), has no means of enforcing the Madrid Protocol for the protection of the Antarctic environment if nations choose to violate the terms to drill for oil or mine for minerals. In addition, she asserts, the growing tourist industry in Antarctica is a danger to the environment. Belkin concludes that

Janet Belkin, "Can Antarctica Be Preserved?" *Carnegie Council for Ethics in International Affairs*, January 8, 2008. Copyright © 2008 Carnegie Council for Ethics in International Affairs. A Carnegie Ethics Online Column, posted on the Web Site of Carnegie Council for Ethics in International Affairs: www.carnegiecouncil.org. Reproduced by permission.

to protect Antarctica's environment, the United Nations must take a more active role in governance. Belkin is a lawyer who teaches classes in international business and law.

As you read, consider the following questions:

1. How is Antarctica unique among the continents, according to Belkin?

2. What two points does the United States' 2,000-mile ice highway connect, according to Belkin?

3. How much of Antarctica does Australia claim, according to the author?

With the November 2007 sinking of the cruise ship *Explorer* in the waters off Antarctica, the fate of this pristine continent has once again been pushed into the public eye. While it is generally acknowledged that mankind has an ethical responsibility to preserve this planet and, in doing so, to protect non-human life, there are differences of opinion as to the degree of such an ethical obligation. These differences become particularly pronounced when dealing with certain "ethical dilemmas," such as using animals for laboratory testing, overuse of fossil fuels, the killing of animals for sport or fashion, bioprospecting that upsets established eco-systems, to name only a few. What seems clear today—especially in light of the *Explorer* disaster—is that one of the greatest ethical dilemmas currently facing the nations of the world is how and to what extent mankind should regulate the vast region of Antarctica.

Antarctica's History

Scientists theorize that approximately 300 million years ago our Earth had only one land mass—later named Pangaea (Greek for "all land"). Shortly thereafter this split into two land bodies. About 200 million years ago the more southern of the two, Gondwanaland, divided into what are now Africa, Australia, South America, the Indian sub-continent, and Antarctica. Prior to the division of Gondwanaland, and prior to the "icing" of the continent, Antarctica was much closer to the equator and was lush with tropical rain forests and populated with dinosaurs. Thus, it is assumed that many of the minerals found in the more northern "sister continents"—including coal, tin, uranium, and oil—will also be found in Antarctica.

Attention was first drawn to these potential resources during the 1957–58 International Geophysical Year (IGY). At that time Antarctica was viewed as a cold, barren, and forbidding place. Today it has a growing number of scientific research bases, ice highways and runways, and—during the 2006–2007 Antarctic Summer—some 30,000 tourists. Despite this growth in research and tourism, Antarctica is unique in that it has no governing body, no electorate (or citizens), and no permanent human inhabitants. Since 1961 it has been regulated by the requirements of the Antarctic Treaty, which gives control of the continent to the 27 states that hold territorial claims, or have established research expeditions, and/or were charter signatories of the treaty. In addition, 17 countries, known as Acceding Parties, have become signatories without a vote, and have agreed to uphold the terms and principles of the treaty. The original Antarctic Treaty has been expanded through additional protocols to create what is now the Antarctic Treaty System (ATS).

The ATS is unique in that it attempts to regulate a land mass with no population and no assertion of territorial sovereignty. Its major aims are to:

- Ensure that Antarctica will be used only for peaceful purposes

- Maintain freedom of scientific investigation

- Share all information relating to research, whether completed or in the planning stage

- Prohibit nuclear explosions and disposal of radioactive waste.

Another important section includes the agreement of seven claimant countries (with overlapping territorial claims) not to seek enforcement of their claims as long as the ATS is effective. However, the United States and Russia (then the USSR) have reserved the right to exert future territorial claims.

The Purpose of the Madrid Protocol

The ATS does include a protocol on environmental protection (known as the Madrid Protocol, agreed to in 1991) designed to protect Antarctica from drilling and/or mining for the mineral resources scientists now believe to exist. The Madrid Protocol requires an environmental assessment of planned activities pursuant to the "scientific research" umbrella. It must be remembered that such an assessment is the responsibility of the state whose nationals are undertaking the research *or* of the state on whose claimed territory such research is being carried out. This is just one instance where territorial claims, although not being pressed, are very much in the forefront. If such research is being undertaken by a state that is not an ATS signatory, then there is really no way for the ATS to exert jurisdiction in order to enforce the requirement of the environmental impact statement. Thus, the claimant state is left with the responsibility to initiate an assessment. However, this is impractical given that assertion of territorial rights would in itself be in violation of the ATS and might very well lead to the destruction of the treaty system.

One must also remember that "research" is a broad category, undefined and unlimited within the treaty, and only time will tell whether the protocol will be able to protect the environment. To further complicate matters, such interpretation and enforcement of the treaty is left to the signatories themselves. Each of the 44 signatories is responsible for policing its citizens; and there is no mechanism for enforcing the terms of the ATS against non-signatory states or their citizens. At present, for example, the Russians are planning to drill within Lake Vostok, one of the fresh water lakes found in the interior of the continent—ostensibly for scientific purposes, but it is easy to imagine that this is really a form of "bio-prospecting" that could lead to future commercial enterprises. Although there have been numerous objections, there is not, under the treaty, any authority that can deny Russia the right to drill and take samples as part of its research program. In addition, the United States has built and maintains a 2,000 mile ice highway from its base at McMurdo Sound to the South Pole; the Australians have enlarged their landing strip to accommodate larger, heavier aircraft; and the weather station established by Stanford University permits its ice runway to be used by the Patriot Hills Base Camp, a tent camp for adventure seeking tourists during the Antarctic Summer.

Tourism in Antarctica Is Self-Regulated

Tourism is not covered by the ATS and, if regulated at all, it is self-regulated by the International Association of Antarctic Tour Operators (IAATO)—a voluntary group. The organization prescribes strict rules for environmental protection and limits the number of passengers disembarking at any one landing site at a given time. There are also detailed rules designated to prevent changes in the native plant and animal life. These include a prohibition against removing any matter from the land and a requirement that the indigenous inhabitants, penguins, have the right of way. Nevertheless, most scientists believe that it is difficult, if not impossible, to completely control the ingress [entering] and egress [leaving] of foreign bodies and plant life. For example, since tourism has increased so dramatically, the penguin population has decreased. (Although it is known that penguins do not fear humans, the relationship between increased tourism and a declining penguin birth rate remains unclear.) Further, because the IAATO is a voluntary organization, a company does not have to be a member in order to operate in Antarctica, and enforcement of the rules means exclusion of the violating company from the organization, not from operating on the continent. This seems a small price to pay if a violation is in the financial interest of the tour operator or cruise ship.

One must applaud the cooperative nature of the ATS. This appears even more surprising when one recalls that the Antarctic Treaty was drafted and approved during a time of intense global stress. To date, the treaty has been reasonably successful in controlling activities on the continent, with one notable exception—the continued hunting and capturing of krill in Antarctic waters by Japanese and Chilean fisherman. Since krill are a major part of the food chain for penguins, this may have a grave effect on the future of these birds.

On the plus side, despite the discovery of coal on the continent and the knowledge that other valuable minerals exist as well, there has been no attempt to drill for them to date. Also, the fact that Antarctica has become one of the "in" places to visit has not yet turned it into a resort area. Still, we must keep in mind that at the time the treaty was originally signed the world's oil supply was deemed to be endless, environmental issues were minimal, and the Cold War superpowers were too occupied with military technology and strategy to focus on the ice-laden continent. Similarly, tourism in general was limited to a select group of affluent travelers, and Antarctica was a place of little practical or tourist interest. The world, however, has changed drastically over the past four-plus decades, and much of what seemed unlikely or impossible in 1961 is commonplace today.

Pressure on the Antarctic Treaty System

Because of the growing interest in the continent, it is necessary to look closely at the ATS in order to ascertain exactly how much protection it will provide now and in the future.

Multilateral Political Cooperation Among Nations Must Supplement the Antarctic Treaty System

The Antarctic Treaty System, originating in 1959, developed under very different circumstances than exist today. It began at a time when a handful of nations were involved in the economic uses of Antarctica, with these uses centering upon scientific research and the attainment of political stability while still protecting the Antarctic environment. The global characteristics of the present Antarctic political and economic agenda are now very different. The "cold war" between the Soviet Union and the United States is over; the sovereign territorial claims of seven nations in Antarctica have been successfully muted by the moratorium on claims to sovereignty that was part of the original treaty; and global commercial interests are threatening to replace scientific research and peace as the primary orientation of the treaty system. At the same time, effective political multilateralism among nations, at least on environmental issues, is on the decline while economic globalization is expanding.

Although globalization yields many economic benefits, there is nonetheless a very real risk that such benefits may be offset by the economic costs resulting from a deterioration of the commons and natural resources of the last undeveloped and pristine continent on Earth. Selecting the appropriate policies to protect this Antarctic environment, and especially as an engine of the global atmospheric and oceanic commons, is extremely important....

Bernard P. Herber, "Issues of Concern and Policy Options for the Antarctic Commons,"
Protecting the Antarctic Commons:
Problems of Economic Efficiency, *Undall Center for Studies in Public Policy, 2007, pp. 61–62.*

As mentioned, the ATS is a voluntary agreement, and as such there is no entity with the power to enforce compliance. The situation is further complicated by the ambivalent feeling of some of the signatories. . . .

In addition, concern about the possibility of an entity seeking mineral resources in Antarctica has become more pressing as existing resources either continue to diminish or become less accessible due to changing political circumstance. The growth of new technology will likely provide less expensive, more efficient ways of locating and extracting these resources. Since the parties that now claim territorial rights have not abandoned those claims but have merely put them on hold, these same parties might choose to reassert their claims should the extraction of valuable minerals become more feasible.

Consider, for example, the following hypothetical scenario as to what might happen should a non-signatory country (or citizen thereof) opt to drill for minerals in Antarctica on land claimed by the United Kingdom. Once it was recognized that such drilling was about to begin, the signatories would become alarmed about this clear violation of the Madrid Protocol and would, most likely, attempt to convince the violator that this would be 1) a blatant violation of the ATS, and 2) a step toward the destruction of Antarctica as we know it. If the violator remained unconvinced, or unconcerned, there would not be much more that the parties to the ATS could do as a body. However, if the violator was, as was suggested, pursuing the project on land claimed by the United Kingdom, and the United Kingdom believed that such drilling would have an excellent chance of success, it seems unlikely that it would just sit back and watch its territory invaded and damaged for someone else's gain. As reported in the *Christian Science Monitor* (August 3, 2006), Australian Conservative MP Barnaby Jones declared upon returning from Antarctica:

"What you have to ask is, do I turn my head and allow another country to exploit my resources, or do I position myself in such a way that I'm going to exploit it myself before they get here?"

(It should be noted that Australia is claiming 42 percent of Antarctica.)

Under such circumstances, an obvious next step might be to declare the drilling to have caused the ATS to be deemed no longer effective, thus enabling the U.K. to pursue its own territorial claim. As other signatories followed suit, one can easily image the chaos that would ensue.

It seems fair to say, then, that there are real problems ahead for the continued reliance upon the ATS as the primary means for protecting Antarctica. The treaty worked well when its main purpose was to keep military bases and nuclear testing off the continent. But when the protections against commercial inroads begin to weaken—whether as a result of biological discoveries, tourism, or the desire for minerals—something stronger and more enforceable is required.

Antarctica's Future

Antarctica is a major link to our planet's geophysical history. It is one of the last unspoiled places—ruled by nature, not by man. If it is to be preserved, we must ensure that the continent remains a laboratory for all—unmarred by environmental, ecological, or political issues. We must understand the future threats to the current system of self-regulation and devise a better way to combat those threats.

I have visited the continent on four occasions and, unfortunately, each successive visit revealed subtle but real changes. There is now a souvenir shop on the former British base at Port Lockroy; the Argentinean base (once a small three person "shack") now serves tea and cookies to visitors; and the American base at Palmer Station has become closed to visitors and no longer allows its scientists to visit the cruise ships because the demand has become too great. There is even talk of building a hotel for tourists, which would inevitably include building additional landing facilities so that tourists could arrive by air rather than, as they do now, by ship. I am not suggesting that tourism be eliminated but, rather, hope that it can be controlled in a manner that will ensure that tourists are regulated visitors rather than demanding consumers. The sinking of the *Explorer* is a clear example of the hazards that increased tourism can bring. We cannot yet assess the effect that even this one calamity will have on the eco-system of Antarctic waters.

Joint United Nations and ATS Governance

Looking forward, one possible avenue for preventing further deterioration of the continent might be to have an organization such as the United Nations assume the enforcement part of the equation. The ATS could remain as a free standing, independent, multilateral treaty. But instead of violations being an issue among the signatories and their nationals, the United Nations could provide the added dimension of enforceability and credibility. This arrangement could be structured such that the UN did not have primary control of the governance of Antarctica. The ATS members would continue to monitor compliance, but treatment of violators would be handled by the UN. Enforcement could take the form of embargoes or even confiscation of machinery and tools used for the activities deemed to be in violation of the ATS. The United Nations Convention on the Law of the Sea (UNCLOS) is frequently brought up as an example of an international treaty that "works," but it must be remembered that UNCLOS does have the enforcement power of the United Nations behind it.

Tourism issues could also be better policed, and compliance with the IAATO guidelines needs stronger enforcement as well. Although IAATO has done a reasonable job of designing a system of self-regulation, some structure needs to be put in place that would require all vessels (tourist or otherwise) entering Antarctic waters to comply with predetermined guidelines. This would hold true whether or not the vessel operators were members of IAATO or nationals of signatory parties. The United Nations, which already includes the International Maritime Organization, might be the best body for enforcement of such a law as well.

In short, involving an international organization in the governance of Antarctica, although perhaps less than ideal, seems a more realistic way of keeping the ATS in place and [more] effective than would permitting it to continue with no enforcement capability. In 2005 the United Nations reviewed the situation in Antarctica as it has been doing, at the request of Malaysia, every three years. At that time it concluded that the ATS was in place and that there was nothing more for the United Nations to do. I believe that this was a grave mistake and one that should be reversed. Perhaps now is the time to begin to organize to such an end. Hopefully our grandchildren shall know an Antarctica that differs very slightly from the one of today—or of 50 million years ago.

*"The [Russian] publicity stunt of plant-
ing a flag on the ocean floor of the
North Pole brought attention to what
could prove to be the most important
territorial dispute of the 21st century."*

Territorial Claims Threaten the Arctic

Adam Wolfe

*In the following viewpoint, Adam Wolfe describes the Russian
planting of a flag on the ocean floor under the North Pole—an
attempted claim for territory that might prove to be oil rich.
Wolfe argues that other nations, such as Canada and the United
States, also will join the fray over competing territorial claims as
global warming melts Arctic ice, making the region and its natural resources more accessible. According to Wolfe, such territorial
claims could lead to conflict that would threaten the Arctic environment. Wolfe is a senior analyst with the* Power and Interest
News Report.

As you read, consider the following questions:

1. How many tons of the Arctic ice sheet are being lost each year, according to a recent study in *Science* magazine?

2. Where is Hans Island, and how does it relate to the territorial claims in the Arctic?

3. According to Wolfe, who has the best claim to the Northwest Passage?

On Aug. 2 [2007], after being escorted by a nuclear-powered icebreaker and another research vessel, two Russian mini-submarines traveled more than two miles below the ice at the North Pole and planted a titanium Russian flag in the seafloor, claiming the underwater territory for Moscow. The publicity stunt played to huge audiences in the Russian media and on state-run television, where the tone of the coverage resembled that given to Soviet cosmonauts. Elsewhere, the underwater mission was greeted with a mixture of humor and anxiety.

Late night talk shows worried what the land grab would mean for Santa's village and his elves, and even Canada's foreign affairs minister, Peter MacKay, mocked the Russian mission. "This isn't the 15th century. You can't go . . . just plant flags and say, 'We're claiming this territory,'" MacKay told CTV.

An Important Territorial Dispute

Whatever the scientific merits of the Russian exploration, the publicity stunt of planting a flag on the ocean floor of the North Pole brought attention to what could prove to be the most important territorial dispute of the 21st century.

As global warming melts the Arctic ice cap, it will provide access to new shipping lanes and make large reserves of natural resources recoverable. A recent study published in *Science* magazine estimated that Greenland and Antarctica are losing a combined total of 125 billion tons of ice sheet each year, and many believe that September could soon be an ice-free month in the Arctic. Some studies estimate a quarter of the world's oil and gas reserves lay below the Arctic ice, but no country has a solid claim to the majority of the territory.

Most of the countries with shorelines along the Arctic Ocean—Russia, Canada, the United States, Denmark, Norway, Sweden, Iceland, and Finland—are looking to extend their claims into what is, for now, covered in thick ice. Russia's flag might be sunk at the North Pole, but Canada and Denmark are looking to claim that seafloor as well.

Proving Land Claims

Every nation is entitled to an exclusive economic zone up to 200 miles from its shoreline under the United Nations Convention on the Law of the Sea, but the rules governing territorial claims to the sea beyond this remain in dispute. The convention gives signatories additional time to make a scientific claim to the areas beyond their allocated zones, which has resulted in many scientific missions around the Arctic ice cap. Russia has until 2009 to prove its claim. Canada, which signed the treaty later, has until 2013.

The Russian mission was aimed at proving that the seabed beneath the North Pole, known as the Lomonosov Ridge, is an extension of the Eurasian continental shelf, and thus falls under Russian control. Russia put this claim to the U.N. [United Nations] Commission on the Limits of the Continental Shelf in 2001, but the panel ruled that there was not sufficient data to support the assertion. Canada and Denmark are also pursuing scientific proof that the ridge is connected to Ellesmere Island and Greenland respectively. They have coordinated research missions over the past two years to counter the Russian claim to the Lomonosov Ridge. A new U.S. Geological Survey mapping of the region is due next year.

Climate Change Could Lead to Regional Tension in the Arctic

"I don't think the Arctic is going to spark World War III, but it's naive to not see Russia militarizing the Arctic," [international affairs expert Scott] Borgerson said.

[U.S. Rear Admiral Arthur E.] Brooks said there have never been any prohibitions on weapons systems there. He downplayed concerns over U.S.-Russian arctic tensions and stressed that despite Moscow's heightened interest in the region, relations are "great." The Russians are just focused on protecting what they view as their territory, he said.

But regional tensions do have the potential to occur, Brooks said. "The worst case scenario is a failure to peacefully settle the arctic boundaries that leads to open conflict between the arctic nations," wrote Brooks in an article. "That threat is not immediate, but could build quickly due to the boundary disputes."

Matthew Rusling,
"Coast Guard Unprepared for Climate Change in Arctic,"
National Defense, vol. 93, no. 657, August 2008.

Nations Flex Their Military Muscles

Not content to rest their claims on scientific merit alone, the countries disputing the sovereignty of the Arctic Ocean are investing in military equipment as well.

Canadian Prime Minister Stephen Harper announced a large investment in his country's arctic fleet. "Canada has a choice when it comes to defending our sovereignty over the Arctic," he said in a July 11 [2007] speech. "We either use it or lose it. And make no mistake, this government intends to use it." He announced the purchase of eight new ice-going patrol boats and an investment in a new port to service them.

Following the Russian flag-planting mission, Harper set off on a three-day tour of Canada's northernmost regions. A spokesman for the prime minister described the purpose of the trip in very clear terms—Harper was there to "reassert Canadian sovereignty" over its Arctic claims. This includes Hans Island, a small, uninhabited island between Ellesmere Island and Greenland that is also claimed by Demark, as well as disputed regions also claimed by the United States.

Russia is also overhauling its arctic fleet and planning additional missions to the region. In March [2007], [Russian] President Putin established the United Shipbuilding Corporation to provide military and civilian ships capable of operating in the frozen north. In case there was any confusion about the ultimate goal of Russia's investment in its arctic fleet, the Murmansk Shipping Company, which operates Russia's icebreaker fleet, recently announced that it would convert one of its nuclear powered icebreakers into an oil-drilling vessel. This followed an announcement that another Russia-sponsored scientific mission to the pole could come as early as November [2007].

The United States' Position

The U.S. position in this competition is complicated. Washington [D.C.] has not signed the U.N. Convention on the Law of the Sea, and thus is not competing to prove that the region falls under U.S. jurisdiction within the U.N. context. Instead it has taken a more unilateral approach, declaring most of the Arctic neutral while defending an expansion of its Alaskan coast. Washington maintains that the Northwest Passage, which is currently commercially navigable for a short window in the summer, is in neutral waters, though Canada claims control of most of the route. Washington is not in a strong position to challenge this right now. It only maintains a small arctic fleet of four icebreakers, two of which are in disrepair.

While the United States does not appear to be competing to claim the North Pole, it does dispute Canada's claim on a portion of the Beaufort Sea, which is thought to contain huge amounts of oil. Canada claims that its economic zone extends 200 miles out along the land border at the 141st meridian, but the United States claims the boundary line between the Alaska and Yukon seafloor should extend out perpendicularly to the coast. The discrepancy in interpretation creates a "wedge" of disputed territory. Both nations have put oil exploration in the disputed region up for bid. Prime Minister Harper's northern tour is, in part, designed to reinforce Canada's claim to the region.

Jostling for Position

The opening of the Arctic is still years away, and growing environmental awareness may help to slow the melting of the polar cap. But the Arctic nations are jostling for position to gain access to riches that could follow the melting ice anyway. Russia has the most robust arctic fleet and the most experience operating in frozen conditions. Canada has the best claim to the Northwest Passage, and is building its capabilities to defend this claim. The United States is not aggressively pursuing control of the region, but with the largest Navy in the world it will not be elbowed out either. Norway's Stateoil probably has the most experience in offshore drilling under arctic conditions, and it would have a lot to gain from moving into the region.

But opening the Northwest Passage or pursuing oil exploration in the Arctic would threaten the region's fragile ecology, and world public opinion of polar bears is far more favorable than that of oil companies. Strict limits on shipping and exploration in the region could ease the growing tensions between the Arctic nations, and commentators have suggested

> *"Increased interest in the Arctic fuelled by economic concerns related to . . . climate change, brings the issue of the region's political control . . . into the spotlight."*

An Arctic Treaty Should Be Established

Rasmus Ole Rasmussen

In the following viewpoint, Rasmus Ole Rasmussen argues that competing territorial claims are likely to cause problems in the Arctic, and that consequently, a treaty similar to the Antarctic Treaty System ought to be established to govern the Arctic regions. He also points to the Svalbard Treaty, an agreement that affects a Norwegian-claimed portion of the Arctic, as a good model. Finally, he asserts that the Arctic Council could form the treaty. Rasmussen is a senior research fellow at the Nordic Center for Spatial Development.

As you read, consider the following questions:

1. Who were the original signatories of the Svalbard Treaty?

Rasmus Ole Rasmussen, "Time for an Arctic Treaty!" *Journal of Nordregio: People and Politics of the Arctic*, vol. 7, 2007, pp. 10–11. Copyright © 2007 Nordregio. Reproduced by permission.

2. According to Rasmussen, who put forward a draft of an Arctic Treaty in 1991?

3. What are the two primary objectives of the Arctic Council, according to Rasmussen?

Increased interest in the Arctic, fuelled by economic concerns related to the ongoing process of climate change, brings the issue of the region's political control and thus of the right to access to the region into the spotlight. The examples of current "hot issues" . . . provide an indication of some of the pressing current questions in need of a legal framework and procedures to best provide for their equitable resolution.

They may however be just the "tip of the iceberg", so one may just as well prepare for a considerable increase in potential conflicts, and start thinking of potential counter measures. But what is most disturbing is the fact that the current discourse seldom makes reference to the population currently residing in the Arctic. In many international settings where the consequences of changes in the Arctic are discussed, the concept of *"Terra Nullius"* [a term from Roman Law meaning "nobody's land"] still seems to be applied.

The Example of the Antarctic Treaty

Two international treaties exist which could be considered as the starting points for the debate. The Antarctic Treaty, which was signed on December 1, 1959, by the 12 countries which were active in Antarctica during the International Geophysical Year 1957–58, when more than 50 Antarctic research stations were established across Antarctica. Secondly, we have the Svalbard Treaty which was signed in Paris on February 9, 1920.

The Antarctic Treaty encompasses all land and ice shelves south of the southern 60th parallel, and the treaty has now been signed by 46 countries. The overall goal of the treaty was to set aside Antarctica as a 'scientific preserve', to establish freedom of scientific investigation, and at the same time ban military activities on the continent. Besides emphasizing Antarctica as a basis for research activities, article 1 of the treaty stresses the need to use Antarctica for peaceful purposes only, prohibiting military activities, while article 4 states that the treaty does not recognize, dispute, or establish territorial sovereignty claims, just as it is emphasized that no new claims would be asserted as long as the treaty is in force.

The majority of Antarctica is claimed by one or more countries, but most countries do not explicitly recognize those claims. Today there are 46 treaty member nations with 28 consultative and 18 acceding members.

The consultative—and thereby voting—members include the seven nations that claim portions of Antarctica as national territory, while the remaining 21 non-claimant nations either do not recognize the claims of others, or have not expressed their positions.

These claims, however, have not thus far led to conflicting situations which have been interpreted as violations of the original ideas behind the treaty to such a degree that it has called for the withdrawal of members.

First and foremost, the ban on military activities seems thus far to have prevented both nuclear weapons and "star wars" installations being sited on the continent.

The Svalbard Treaty and Norway's Claims

The Svalbard Treaty concerns the Archipelago of Spitsbergen and Björnö, and is based on recognition of the sovereignty of Norway over the Archipelago, while at the same time ensuring that these territories should be provided with an equitable regime which would ensure their development and peaceful utilisation.

The original signatories include Australia, Canada, Denmark, France, Italy, Japan, the Netherlands, Norway, Sweden, the United Kingdom and the United States, while The Soviet

Union signed in 1924 and Germany in 1925. Today there are now over 40 signatories. All signatories have been given equal rights to engage in commercial activities, for instance coal mining, as well as equal fishing rights near the Spitsbergen Archipelago.

Norway has sought exclusive rights to the area since 1977. The treaty, however, emphasizes that Norway shall be free to maintain, take or decree suitable measures to ensure the preservation and, if necessary, the re-constitution of the *fauna* and *flora* of the regions, as well as the territorial waters. Besides discussing regulation measures in relation to resources, the concept of peaceful utilization has also been debated, as the Treaty allows the signatories to establish and maintain those installations needed in connection with communication, weather forecasts etc., installations which may also serve military purposes.

The situation has however never been so heated that it has led to real conflict situations, as the Norwegians have managed to maintain the spirit of the treaty intact.

A Draft of an Arctic Treaty

A draft of an Arctic Treaty was put forward in 1991 by Donat Pharand, Professor Emeritus of International Law, University of Ottawa. He emphasized the idea of an Arctic Region Council aiming at regional cooperation which should lead to the use of the Arctic Region for peaceful purposes. In this connection he stressed seven main points as being important for this:

1. to facilitate regional cooperation generally among its Members;

2. to ensure the protection of the environment;

3. to promote the co-ordination of scientific research;

4. to encourage the conservation and appropriate management of living resources;

Competing Claims: Nations of the Arctic Region

ARCTIC REGION

TAKEN FROM: www.lib.utexas.edu, 2007.

5. to foster economic and sustainable development;

6. to further the health and social well-being of the indigenous and other inhabitants of the Arctic Region; and

7. to promote the use of the Arctic Region for peaceful purposes.

Oran Young, Professor at the University of California and a long time writer on issues in relation to governance issues and the Arctic, stresses how a substantial number of "soft" agreements, for instance in connection with environmental protection issues etc., already show a legacy of both means and measures available in the existing laws and regulations when it comes to specific problems.

He also underlines the fact that on a more general level there are limitations to how existing Arctic governance systems can be structured to minimize problems arising from gaps and overlaps. He therefore raises the question to what extent 'added value' would result from the creation of legally binding international arrangements for the Arctic, and what the proper relationship between international institutions and organizations in the Arctic might be.

The Role of the Arctic Council

In 1998 the Arctic Council was established as a forum for co-operation in the Arctic. In addition to the eight states with sovereignty over territory in the Arctic—Canada, Denmark, Finland, Iceland, Norway, Russia, Sweden and the United States—the Council included a number of organizations representing indigenous people as Permanent Participants. They do not vote, but otherwise participate fully in the work of the organization.

Similarly a number of non-governmental organizations and representatives from other countries are also present at these meetings. They may also participate in project activities arranged by the Council.

The Council has two primary objectives. First, to promote environmental protection which has been a major issue among the Arctic nations since the establishment of the Arctic Environmental Protection Strategy in 1991—aiming at addressing environmental issues affecting the entire region. Secondly, it is to promote sustainable development in the Arctic, emphasizing the special economic circumstances of the indigenous people and other residents of the Arctic in relation to the preservation of the environment.

To these ends, the Council has endorsed a number of co-operative activities to be carried out primarily through a series of subsidiary bodies. The structure of the Council, however, is generally seen more as a forum for exchange of opinions and ideas than as an organization establishing binding agreements and resolving conflicts. This provides for an open and informal forum for the development of project activities relevant for the Arctic residents. At the same time, it limits very much the potential of the organization to establish binding solutions.

Two Major Challenges for an Arctic Treaty

The suggestions and the legacy therefore leave the Arctic—and any treaties addressing the future of the Arctic—with two major challenges. This is to develop a treaty which will enable the population already living in the Arctic to become active and decisive members of an organisation which will be very influential in respect of their future lives. Also it is to learn from the two treaties mentioned above, stressing the need to use the Arctic for peaceful purposes only.

> *"Overall, Canada's Arctic land and maritime claims are fairly solid and well recognized."*

Canada Has Legal Claims to Arctic Territory and Waters

François Côté and Robert Dufresne

In the following viewpoint, François Côté and Robert Dufresne review Canada's territorial and maritime claims in the Arctic. They argue that Canada's claims are based on occupation of the land as well as the granting of the northern territories by the United Kingdom. Further, they assert that the Northwest Passage is a Canadian internal waterway and is thus subject to Canadian jurisdiction, despite the fact that the United States claims that it is an international waterway. In sum, the writers argue that Canadian claims are strong and legal. Côté and Dufresne are writers for the Parliamentary Information and Research Service of Canada's Library of Parliament.

As you read, consider the following questions:

1. How big is Hans Island and who lives there, according to the writers?

Francois Côté and Robert Dufresne, "Canada's Legal Claims Over Arctic Territory and Waters," *Parliamentary Information and Research Service*, December 2007. Reproduced with the permission of the Library of Parliament, 2009.

2. What is the most important and authoritative maritime law treaty, according to the writers?

3. What is the Northwest Passage, and how does Canada claim it, according to the viewpoint?

Canada has exclusive sovereignty rights, authority and privileges in relation to the land masses of the Arctic Archipelago. Accordingly, it can apply and enforce its laws, regulate the conduct of activities, and exclude aliens and foreign nationals who would enter its territory without permission.

The Legal Basis for Canada's Claim to Arctic Territory

The legal basis for Canadian sovereignty over these islands rests predominantly on a mix of cession [a legal term meaning that the land has been ceded to the country by its former owner] and occupation, to which considerations of self-determination could be added. More specifically, cession refers to grants of northern territory by the United Kingdom; occupation involves Canada's activities on Arctic islands since cession took place and, in particular, on those islands over which multiple sovereignty claims overlap; and self-determination concerns the will of the inhabitants of the Arctic islands to be governed under Canadian institutions.

While the claim to territory by way of cession may be valid, an effective occupation claim by Canada is complicated by the fact that, given the challenges of this remote environment, human activity in the Arctic Archipelago has been limited. Nevertheless, Canadian territorial sovereignty enjoys enduring recognition and acquiescence from other states, which makes Canada's claim extremely robust from a legal standpoint. Accordingly, Canadian sovereignty over the Arctic islands is legally uncontroversial, and any concerns that Canada is not sufficiently present and active to fulfill the principle of occupation are unlikely to weaken its claim. Its claim would be undermined only if Canada were to abandon the territory completely, or if it were to tolerate the effective presence of another state in the Arctic islands as a competing sovereign.

The Case of Hans Island

The case of Hans Island is the exception to Canada's accepted sovereignty over the Arctic islands. Hans Island is situated in the centre of the Kennedy Channel of Nares Strait, between Canada's Ellesmere Island and Greenland, a territory of Denmark. Only 1.3 square kilometres in area, it is uninhabited. Canada and Denmark both claim the island as their own.

A 1973 agreement between Canada and Denmark on the delimitation of their respective continental shelves deliberately excludes Hans Island in the absence of a settlement over sovereignty. Since the mid-2000s Canada and Denmark have both reasserted their sovereignty over the disputed island through on-site visits. In September 2005, the two countries issued a joint statement declaring that "we will continue our efforts to reach a long-term solution to the Hans Island dispute." But neither country has abandoned its claim, and the dispute remains unresolved.

The stakes in the dispute are relatively limited in geographical terms: they concern territorial sovereignty over the island itself and will have an impact on the size of the respective maritime zones for the region left open in the 1973 agreement. Some Canadian commentators, however, see the question of sovereignty over Hans Island as having broader implications for keeping intact Canada's claim over the Arctic islands, and thus strengthening its resistance against any challenges.

Canada's Maritime Claims

Title to Arctic territory comes with an important advantage, i.e., the capacity to claim, as a coastal state, rights in relation to the waters in which the islands sit. The nature and extent of those rights are provided, among others, in the 1982 *United Nations Convention on the Law of the Sea* (UNCLOS), the most important and authoritative maritime law treaty. Waters bordering on territory are divided into maritime zones, in which states are able to claim and exercise more or less extensive sets of rights.

Maritime zones are measured or determined from baselines that mark the end of a state's territory and the beginning of its maritime extension. Normally, baselines closely follow the coast at the low-tide line, but in cases where the coast is severely indented with numerous small bays, states can draw straight baselines to simplify the delineation. Waters on the landward side of the straight baselines are considered internal waters, although a right of passage sometimes exists in such circumstances. Canada's claim to Arctic maritime zones is based on the straight baseline method. A simplifying line is drawn around the Arctic Archipelago, and the maritime zones claimed are measured from that line onward.

Canadian Internal Waters and a Twelve-Mile Territorial Sea Limit

According to Canada's application of the straight baseline method, waters within the baseline at the external edge of the Archipelago are Canadian internal waters—a claim that has been contested, as explained below, in relation to the Northwest Passage. Under international law, a state is fully sovereign over such [internal] waters and can therefore fully apply and enforce its laws over persons, goods and incidents therein. It can also exclude any foreigner or foreign ship from those waters.

Seaward from the straight baseline is a 12-mile territorial zone surrounding the Arctic Archipelago. In that zone, Canada has the capacity to prevent the commission of an offence under its federal customs, fiscal, immigration or sanitary law and the capacity to enforce such law through power of arrest, search and seizure. Under international law, a state's sovereignty over its 12-mile territorial zone (including its waters, air space, seabed and subsoil) is subject to an important exception: the right of innocent passage enjoyed by ships of all states, i.e., the right to transit through the waters toward the coast of the state or toward the high sea, without engaging in activities disruptive to peace and order. Importantly, commercial navigation usually qualifies as an appropriate exercise of the right of innocent passage; submarines may also pass through territorial waters, although they must surface to do so.

The Exclusive Economic Zone and the Continental Shelf

Pursuant to UNCLOS, Canada has a 200-nautical-mile (370 km) Exclusive Economic Zone (EEZ) around the Arctic Archipelago. Under UNCLOS and Canadian law, coastal state jurisdiction and sovereign rights in an EEZ are for the purpose of exploring and exploiting, conserving and managing the natural resources of the waters (including living and non-living resources), the seabed and its subsoil, and rights of economic exploitation of the zone (e.g., the mining of energy resources).

Canada also claims rights in its continental shelf. Under the 1997 *Oceans Act* and in accordance with Article 76 of UNCLOS, the default length of Canada's continental shelf extends to 200 nautical miles from the straight baselines, but it is also possible to claim an extended continental shelf if scientific evidence can be provided that the shelf beyond the 200 miles is indeed a geological extension of the continent.... With respect to the continental shelf, coastal states enjoy sovereign rights of exploration and exploitation of mineral and other non-living natural resources of the seabed and subsoil and of living organisms belonging to sedentary species. However, un-

Canada Claims Jurisdiction over the Canadian Arctic

"As an environmental matter, as a security matter and as an economic matter we are making it perfectly clear that not only do we claim jurisdiction over the Canadian Arctic, we are also going to put the full resources of the government of Canada behind enforcing that jurisdiction," [Canadian Prime Minister Stephen] Harper said.

"Canada Requires Ship Registration in Arctic,"
USA Today, *August 27, 2008.*

like EEZ rights, the rights in the continental shelf do not include rights to fisheries and other living resources in the water column above the seabed.

Canada's Environmental Protection Authority in the Arctic

Canada asserts environmental protection powers in relation to its Arctic maritime zones through various Acts. The 1970 *Arctic Waters Pollution Prevention Act* establishes waste disposal as an offence, a corresponding regime of civil liability, regulatory powers related to shipping safety control zones and ship construction standards, and enforcement powers. The Act applies to the waters between specific eastern and western lines and waters contiguous (up to 100 nautical miles) with land north of the 60th parallel. Moreover, environmental protection powers related to Canada's maritime zones in general are also applicable in Arctic waters. . . .

Canada's Disputed Arctic Maritime Claims

Although Canada's Arctic maritime claims are not contested for the most part by the international community, two related issues have been controversial and remain disputed: the status of the Northwest Passage, and the delimitation of the Beaufort Sea. In addition, claims over the continental shelf in the Arctic circumpolar region may prove to be an area of dispute between Canada and other states as they articulate the bases for their claims more precisely.

The Northwest Passage is a maritime path comprising up to seven routes, of which two are the main ones, connecting the Davis Strait and Baffin Bay in the east to the Bering Strait in the west. Canada considers that it is sovereign over the waters of the Northwest Passage on the ground that they are internal waters. It invokes two legal bases in support of its position: the waters are internal (1) by virtue of historic title, and/or (2) by virtue of their being on the landward side of straight baselines drawn around the entire Arctic Archipelago in 1985. To be clear, historic title enables a state to supersede purely geographical considerations in claiming sovereignty and to prevent the application of the rules and principles concerning the territorial sea, the EEZ or the high seas that would otherwise negatively affect its consideration of the maritime area in question as being entirely within its domestic jurisdiction. Three conditions must be present for historic title to exist: (1) exclusive exercise of state jurisdiction; (2) a long lapse of time; and (3) acquiescence by foreign states.

Canada's claim to the Northwest Passage according to these two legal bases has been extensively analysed. For the most part, the historic title argument is considered to be weak. Instead, the straight baseline argument is thought to be better and strong enough in international law. With the Northwest Passage deemed part of Canadian internal waters, Canada would be able to regulate activities therein and to enforce its laws in the Passage, while foreign states and ships would enjoy no maritime rights under international law.

The United States Protests

However, Canada's characterization of the Northwest Passage as Canadian internal waters is contested. The United States, the most vocal disputant, considers that the Passage qualifies as an international strait. Under international law, a strait must meet a geographical and a functional requirement to be considered international. The geographical requirement is that it must be a water corridor between adjacent land masses that links two bodies of the high seas or other waters. The functional requirement is that it be used as a route for international maritime traffic. If a strait meets these two requirements and is thus international in the legal sense, foreign states have navigation rights, or right of transit, through the strait—which means that they do not have to request permission to navigate through it.

Some observers consider the US argument to be weak, given that the Passage has seldom been used for international traffic. However, maritime traffic through the Passage is predicted to increase as it becomes more accessible as a result of climate change and the melting of the Arctic sea-ice. Accordingly, some experts have raised the prospect that the Passage would eventually be internationalized, i.e., it would gradually become an international strait. If the international strait qualification were to prevail, Canada would not necessarily lose all rights and powers over the waters of the Passage, but those rights would be diluted insofar as Canada would be obliged to respect the navigational rights of other states.

Other experts have been raising the possibility of a third alternative, namely that the Northwest Passage be considered territorial waters subject to a right of passage. Accordingly, the Passage would not meet the requirements of an international strait, but neither would it be entirely enclosed within Canada's straight baselines. Hence, foreign states would enjoy the right of innocent passage through the Passage. . . .

Water Claims in the Beaufort Sea

The dispute in the Beaufort Sea concerns the maritime extension of the land boundary between Yukon and Alaska. The area is considered to be resource-rich. Canada claims that the maritime boundary runs along the 141st meridian as an extension of the territorial boundary agreed with the United States. However, the United States rejects this position, arguing that the boundary must be determined by using the equidistance principle—a recognized mode of maritime delimitation that traces a line at equal distance from the closest land point of each state. This produces a line that reflects more closely the direction of the respective coast lines. Canada and the United States are in effect both promoting the use of a delimitation method that will best serve their respective interests and that will produce, from each of their perspectives, the largest maritime zone possible. Resolution of this dispute is still pending. . . .

Canada's Arctic Land and Water Claims in Sum

Overall, Canada's Arctic land and maritime claims are fairly solid and well recognized, although some limited elements remain disputed. On the territorial front, Hans Island is the exception to Canada's unchallenged sovereign title to the entire Arctic Archipelago. Although Canadian claims over Arctic waters are also generally very strong, disputes about some of them are more significant both geographically and in terms of their implications for Canada. First, the maritime boundary delimitation in the Beaufort Sea, which remains to be settled, could maintain or restrain the maritime zones that Canada currently claims in that region, including claims over the resources found therein. Second, the extent to which Canada can secure its claim that the waters of the Northwest Passage are internal, as opposed to an international strait or part of its territorial sea, will be significant for Canada—not only in its relationship with the United States but also in relation to other states around the globe wishing to navigate through them. The characterization of the Northwest Passage could have an impact on the extent and conditions of maritime traffic therein, and consequently on resultant pollution and Canada's ability to prevent and manage it. Third, Canada and other Arctic nations are each working on submissions for a claim to an extended continental shelf over the next few years; this exercise carries with it the potential for international disputes as the division of the Arctic seabed for the purposes of resource exploitation and management is settled.

Canada's claims to Arctic sovereignty and rights permit it to respond to opportunities and challenges encountered in the region, including strategic defence issues related to potential incursions into the Canadian Arctic; protection of the environment and the Arctic ecosystems; the preservation of the way of life of Aboriginal peoples; the good governance of local communities; and the exploitation and management of the Arctic's renewable and non-renewable resources. It is anticipated that such opportunities and challenges will be amplified and multiplied in years to come, notably under the impact of climate change; thus, Canada's claims over the Arctic are expected to emerge as a more important dimension of its foreign relations.

> "An accord among the U.S., Canada, and Denmark/Greenland would allow the three nations to exercise rigorous control over shipping through North America's Arctic waters."

The United States, Canada, and Denmark Should Jointly Control Arctic Waters

Dianne DeMille

In the following viewpoint, Dianne DeMille argues that because the United States, Canada, and Denmark are close allies, they should quickly assume joint control of shipping on the North American side of the Arctic to prevent further Russian expansion. She further contends that Canada could continue to claim sovereignty of the Northwest Passage, but that having two partners to help Canada police and clean up the waterway would be to its advantage. Transit fees from ships could pay for the cost of patrolling and cleanup, DeMille concludes. Dianne DeMille is a writer for the Canadian American Strategic Review.

Dianne DeMille, "Steerage and Stewardship: US, Canada, and Denmark/Greenland Should Join Forces to Guard the North American Side of the Arctic," *Canadian American Strategic Review*, September 2008. Reproduced by permission.

As you read, consider the following questions:

1. Where are Canadian and American soldiers fighting shoulder to shoulder, according to DeMille, and how does this point relate to her argument?

2. What agreement is already in place that, according to DeMille, could serve as the nucleus for a more far-reaching regime?

3. What law did Canada pass in 1970 relative to this viewpoint?

The Arctic Ocean is bracketed by two continents: Eurasia and North America. The Arctic coastline of Eurasia is dominated by Russia. On the North American side there are three nation-states busily mapping the ocean floor to put their claims to the UN [United Nations] Commission which will adjudicate the 'Limits of the Continental Shelf'. But the three countries on this side of the Arctic are intimate allies. Take one example: our soldiers are fighting shoulder to shoulder in Southern Afghanistan. Our bilateral boundary disputes within our Arctic are minor as compared with the expansionist claims of Russia.

Would it not make more sense for the US, Canada, and Denmark/Greenland to join together, as soon as possible, to control shipping through the North American side of the Arctic and sort out the national control over the seabed in our own time. All we need from the UN Law of the Sea Commission is the dotted line that will tell Russia: 'This far and no further'.

Northwest Passage—International Waterway *or* a Series of Controlled Shipping Lanes?

In the past, the United States has said that it wants to make the Northwest Passage—which Canada claims as an internal waterway—into a series of 'international straits'. Fortunately,

U.S., Canadian, and Danish Cooperation Is a Good Strategy

As to engaging the United States, Canada needs to act on commonalities that have been slighted in the mutual leeriness that's arisen from our dispute over the Northwest Passage. Fully aware of the Arctic region's opening to cooperation as well as conflict, Canada and the United States ought to recognize and base their collaboration on unexploited opportunities for joint stewardship in Arctic North America.

The range of bilateral hands-on cooperation strategies open to our two countries is very large. The majority should be undertaken with the direct participation of Canadian and US Arctic indigenous peoples. The list includes maritime domain awareness and, in due course, maritime command under NORAD [North American Aerospace Defense Command]; ocean stewardship under the Security and Prosperity Partnership of North America; coast guard cooperation in search and rescue operations, including in the event of a cruise ship fire or grounding; cooperation between other agencies of our two countries if there is a major air disaster; improved capabilities for oil spill cleanup in ice-covered waters; protection of Arctic ice and snow albedo [the albedo of an object is the extent to which it reflects sunlight] against black soot through the joint imposition of commercial vessel smokestack emission controls; . . . and an invitation to the United States and Denmark/Greenland to comment as Canada proceeds to bring the AWPPA [Arctic Waters Pollution Prevention Act] regulations up to date.

Franklyn Griffiths, "Canadian Arctic Sovereignty:
Time to Take Yes for an Answer On the Northwest Passage,"
Northern Exposure: Peoples, Powers and Prospects
for Canada's North, *IRPP, 2008. www.irpp.org.*

the White House and the State Department are currently giving their 'Arctic Policy' a thorough rethink. The new policy will be unveiled in the coming weeks [Fall 2008]. Perhaps some astute State Department official has realized that opening up the Northwest Passage to 'unfettered' international traffic is not the best way to achieve the United States' twin goals: US security in the Arctic, *and* the free movement of US ships—commercial and military.

There is a better solution: Joint jurisdiction over all shipping through the Arctic of the North American continent. This joint jurisdiction could be put into effect by a trilateral treaty among the US, Canada, and Denmark/Greenland. (Greenland is a semi-autonomous province of Denmark, exercising 'Home Rule'.) There is already an agreement in place which could serve as a nucleus for a more far-reaching regime: the 1983 Canada-Denmark 'Agreement for Cooperation relating to the Marine Environment'.

A Trilateral Agreement

An accord among the US, Canada, and Denmark/Greenland would allow the three nations to exercise rigorous control over shipping through North America's Arctic waters. But it would do more. It would address the security concerns of the United States and allow the free passage of US vessels through the Arctic Archipelago.

At the same time, the treaty would maintain Canada's claim to nominal sovereignty over the 'Northwest Passage'. It is true that sharing the jurisdiction over shipping through these straits would somewhat 'soften' the edges of our [Canada's] claim to absolute sovereignty. However, granting free passage to two of Canada's closest allies—should they be willing to share responsibility for policing the channels of the Arctic Archipelago—is far preferable to opening these straits to 'unfettered' traffic from all over the world.

International waterways usually end up as unsalvagable sewers. The spectre of rusty-hulled ships, flying flags-of-convenience, steaming through a fragile Arctic environment unnerves the people who live in Canada's North. A body of water that belongs to everyone, belongs to no one. No one nation will take on the responsibility of policing and clean-up, because there is no incentive to do so. And no one nation has adequate resources for massive clean-ups.

Financing the Scheme

Which brings us to the money: transit fees. The US (Alaska) and Denmark (Greenland) control shipping via the western and eastern approaches to the channels of the Arctic Archipelago. With sufficient revenues from pooled transit fees, the three nations would be able to monitor all ships using the narrow channels of the Arctic Archipelago. Together, the three countries could maintain a contingency fund to carry out any clean up campaign.

In 1970, Canada passed the Arctic Waters Pollution Prevention Act (AWPPA). It became Article 234 of the United Nations Convention of the Law of the Sea. This Article is referred to as the 'Arctic Exception'. The nickname is apt. The Arctic Ocean *is* the exception. And, because it is an exception, the stringent control over the channels of the Archipelago need not be taken as a precedent for any other international straits around the globe.

The Arctic Ocean is *not* equivalent to the Pacific or the Atlantic. It is exceptional, and we must make all efforts required to protect it. Any voyage through an aquatic environment carries inherent risks. Whenever a ship, boat, or submarine pushes through a pristine waterway, there is no such thing as 'innocent passage'.

Periodical Bibliography

The following articles have been selected to supplement the diverse views presented in this chapter.

Terry Collins
"Experts Meet on Need for New Rules to Govern World's Fragile Polar Regions," United Nations University, September 7, 2008. www.eurekalert.org.

Jill Grob
"Antarctica's Frozen Territorial Claims," *Boston College International & Comparative Law Review*, Spring 2007.

Luke Harding
"Kremlin Lays Claim to Huge Chunk of Oil-Rich North Pole," *The Guardian*, June 28, 2007.

Daniel Howden and Ben Holst
"Race for the Arctic," *The Independent*, January 5, 2005.

Maxim Krans
"New Wrestling Bout over the Arctic," *Knight Ridder/Tribune*, October 24, 2007.

P. Whitney Lackenbauer
"Arctic Front, Arctic Homeland: Re-evaluating Canada's Past Record and Future Prospects in the Circumpolar North," Canadian International Council, July 2008. www.canadianinternationalcouncil.org.

Elana Wilson Rowe and Helge Blakkisrud
"A Revival of the Russian North?" *Journal of Nordregio*, vol. 7, no. 4, December 2007.

Azizan Abu Samah and Nasaruddin Abdul Rahman
"Sustaining Malyasia's Interest in Antarctica: From Diplomacy to Science," National Antarctic Research Center, 2007.

John A. Sullivan
"US Company Moving Swiftly with Claims over Arctic Region Energy," *Natural Gas Week*, vol. 24, no. 14, April 7, 2008.

Gerald Traufetter
"The Battle for the North Pole: Melting Ice Brings Competition for Resources," *Der Spiegel*, September 19, 2008.

OPPOSING
VIEWPOINTS®
SERIES

CHAPTER 2

How Does Climate Change Affect the North and South Poles?

Chapter Preface

Many scientists now agree that the Earth is warming because of human activity, most notably through the emission of greenhouse gases. Even those who contest that human activity is not the major agency in global warming do not dispute that the climate is, indeed, changing. The evidence for this is nowhere clearer than at the North and South Poles, where sea ice is melting at a historically unprecedented rate. Thus, according to the International Polar Year 2007–2008, in a statement issued on February 19, 2009, "It is not surprising that one of the main topics of this 4th IPY [International Polar Year] was climate change, since the polar regions play a very important role in Earth's climate."

The rate of warming has opened yet another debate: the "tipping point" scenario. In his article "A Green Tipping Point," appearing in the October 12, 2007, issue of *Time*, Bryan Walsh defines a tipping point as the place "at which the momentum for change becomes unstoppable." Some climatologists believe that the Earth has already passed the tipping point with regard to global warming. They argue that the momentum toward a much warmer Earth has grown so strong that nothing humans can do will reverse the movement. All that can be done is for humans to try to mitigate the damage by drastically cutting greenhouse emissions and preparing to adapt to the change.

Other scientists, while not abandoning the prediction of global warming, do not believe the Earth has passed the tipping point yet. If these scientists are correct, then quickly moving to reduce greenhouse gas emissions might prevent the doomsday scenario painted by those who believe the tipping point has passed.

Still other scientists believe that the idea of tipping points is irrelevant. They believe that the Earth goes through long periods of warming and cooling, through processes unknown. In 1801, the famous British astronomer William Herschel linked sun spots with a warming climate, according to Peter N. Spotts writing in his 2007 *Christian Science Monitor* article "Are Sunspots Prime Suspects in Global Warming?" He also cites Danish researcher Henrik Svensmark's 1997 study suggesting that cosmic rays influence climate on Earth. Other more recent studies also suggest a potential connection.

Finally, other scientists such as John R. Christy, director of the Earth Science System at the University of Alabama at Huntsville, theorize that "it is possible increased warming will be offset by other factors, such as increased cloudiness that would reflect more sunlight," as quoted in a 2006 article by Juliet Eilperin in *The Washington Post*.

So is there a tipping point or not? Writers such as Steve Connor believe there is, and that the Earth has already gone over the edge. Writing in *The Independent* in September 2005, he reports "Scientists fear that the Arctic has now entered an irreversible phase of warming. . . . The greatest fear is that the Arctic has reached a 'tipping point' beyond which nothing can reverse the continual loss of sea ice."

While it is possible to argue for and against the notion of a tipping point, it is difficult not to see climate change as a vital topic for those who live in and those who study the North and South Poles. The writers of the following viewpoints consider the role of climate change from a wide variety of perspectives, offering hypotheses of what the future holds for the polar regions of the world.

> *"During [the next 90 years], the scientists predict that half of the Arctic's summer sea ice will melt. . .which contains enough ice to raise sea level by some 23 feet."*

The Polar Ice Melt Will Cause Ocean Levels to Rise Rapidly

Colin Woodard

In the following viewpoint, Colin Woodard describes the collapse of portions of Antarctica's ice sheet and connects this melting to that occurring in the Arctic. He asserts that, according to scientists, sea levels will rise catastrophically and quickly as a result of the melting polar ice caps. He further notes that indigenous communities in the Arctic already are experiencing devastation as a result of rising seas. Woodard is a journalist and the author of Ocean's Ends: Travels Through Endangered Seas *(2000).*

As you read, consider the following questions:

1. What are the names of the three collapsing Antarctic ice shelves, according to the viewpoint?

Colin Woodard, "The Big Meltdown: Something's Happening at Both Poles," *E/The Environmental Magazine*, March-April 2005, pp. 19–21. Copyright © 2005 Earth Action Network, Inc. Reproduced with permission from *E/The Environmental Magazine*.

2. How much have average Arctic winter temperatures risen in the past fifty years, according to Woodard?

3. According to Woodard, who is Shelia Wats-Cloutier, and what did she urge the George W. Bush administration to do?

When Antarctica's Larsen-B ice shelf—a 10,000-year-old, 650-foot thick expanse of floating ice the size of Rhode Island—collapsed three years ago, Pedro Skvarca had a front-row seat. With the Antarctic Peninsula being swept by an unprecedented summer heat wave in February 2002, Skvarca, a glaciologist with the Argentine Antarctic Institute, jumped in a rugged twin-engine turboprop and flew off from his Antarctic research station to inspect the cliff-like seaward edge of the remote ice shelf.

What he saw, Skvarca recalls, was astonishing. "The surface of the ice shelf was almost totally covered by melt ponds and lakes, and waterfalls were spilling over the top and into the ocean," he says. Great slices of the Larsen-B's leading edge had broken off, filling the Weddell Sea with icebergs and slush. Two weeks later, almost the entire ice shelf had disintegrated. "It was unbelievable to see how fast it had broken up. The coastline hadn't changed for more than 9,000 years and then it changed completely in just a few weeks."

Now scientists studying the aftermath of the collapse say it will very likely have unpleasant implications for the rest of us. The collapse of the Larsen-B and its smaller northern neighbors, the Larsen-A and Wordie ice shelves, in the face of warmer summer temperatures has caused the vast glaciers and ice sheets behind them to begin sliding into the sea at a remarkable pace. Aerial and satellite imagery show that the glaciers behind the Larsen-B increased their seaward flow by two to six times in the months after the ice shelf's collapse, with some of them thinning by more than 100 feet.

Thinning Glaciers Mean Higher Sea Levels

Unlike the floating ice shelves, thinning glaciers contribute to global sea-level rise.

"The glaciers took off like a race horse after the ice shelves were removed," says Ted Scambos, a researcher at the National Snow and Data Center in Boulder, Colorado. "Just a decade ago we glaciologists were talking about gradual changes in glaciers taking place over centuries. Now we're seeing things that we didn't think glaciers could do in terms of their speed of response."

And it's not just happening on the Antarctic Peninsula. Similar studies of glaciers entering the Amundsen Sea, some 1,200 miles away in West Antarctica, show them doubling their flow since the 1990s. This is especially worrying because the glaciers in this area drain the West Antarctic Ice Sheet, a precariously balanced portion of the southern ice cap that contains enough ice to raise sea levels by 20 feet. By comparison, the sea-level rise predictions endorsed by the 2,600 scientists of the Intergovernmental Panel on Climate Change are only about two feet by 2100.

The Arctic Is Warming Rapidly

If anything, the news from the Arctic is even more troubling. In November an international team of 300 scientists completed an unprecedented four-year study of the region that found it is warming at nearly twice the rate of the rest of the planet. Average winter temperatures in much of the region have increased by as much as four to seven degrees Fahrenheit in the past 50 years, and they are expected to warm by another seven to 13 degrees by the end of the century. During that time, the scientists predict that half of the Arctic's summer sea ice will melt, along with much of the Greenland Ice Sheet, which contains enough ice to raise sea level by some 23 feet.

Arctic Sea Ice is Melting Rapidly

September ice extent from 1979 to 2008 shows a thirty-year decline. The September rate of sea ice decline since 1979 has now increased to −11.7 percent per decade.

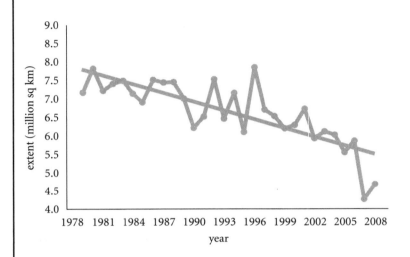

TAKEN FROM: National Snow and Ice Data Center, October 2, 2008. http://nsidc.org/news/press/20081002_seaice_pressrelease.html.

"The preponderance of evidence suggests that the warming of the past 50 years has mostly come from greenhouse gas emissions and everything we're seeing in the Arctic is 100 percent consistent with that," says Robert Corell, a senior fellow at the American Meteorological Society in Washington, D.C. and chairperson of study for the Arctic Climate Impact Assessment.

Inuit Communities Are Washing into the Sea

Arctic people are already feeling the effects of this polar thaw. Several Inuit communities in Canada, Alaska and Russia are washing into the sea because the sea ice that used to dampen waves is vanishing. The area covered by sea ice has shrunk by more than six percent since 1978. And in the central Arctic, submarine measurements indicate that the average thickness has declined by 40 percent in recent decades. If trends continue, scientists warn that polar bears, seals and other animals northern people rely on will be driven towards extinction.

Until recently, many parts of the Arctic were more accessible in winter, when ice roads made truck transport possible. But warmer temperatures are turning those roads into impassable tracks of mud for more and more of the year. Over the past 30 years, the Alaskan Department of Natural Resources has been forced to halve the number of ice road travel days from 200 to 100. In northern Russia, melting permafrost has damaged roads, railways, apartment buildings and airport runways and ruptured several oil and gas pipelines.

A Grim Future for Coastal Areas

In Iceland and Greenland, glaciers have been in rapid retreat, with the Greenland ice sheet experiencing summertime surface melting over 16 percent more of its surface area since 1979. "Greenland is melting much more rapidly in the past two or three years than anyone imagined possible" Corell says. "The ice is so bad in eastern Greenland that people are killing their sled dogs because they cannot hunt enough seal to keep them."

After the report's release, Shelia Watt-Cloutier, the Nunavut, Canada-based chairperson of the Inuit Circumpolar Conference, traveled to Washington to urge the Bush administration to take global warming seriously. "By looking at what is already happening in remote Inuit villages in Alaska . . . you can understand the future dangers for more populated areas of the world such as Florida, Louisiana or California," she told a Senate committee hearing. "Use us in the Arctic as your early warning system."

> "*[Former Vice President] Al Gore's claim that ocean levels will rise 20 feet thanks to global warming seems to ignore the laws of thermodynamics.*"

The Polar Ice Melt Will Not Cause Ocean Levels to Rise Rapidly

Jerome J. Schmitt

In the following viewpoint, mechanical engineer Jerome J. Schmitt uses mathematical calculations to argue that the laws of thermodynamics demonstrate that global warming cannot generate enough heat to melt the Polar ice caps at a sufficient rate to cause rapid sea-level rise. Schmitt asserts that if sea level rise occurs at all, it will not happen for some 3,000 years as opposed to the 100 years claimed by those who believe the climate is warming rapidly. Schmitt is president of NanoEngineering Corporation, located in West Palm Beach, Fla.

As you read, consider the following questions:

1. According to Schmitt, what is the only source of energy to heat the Earth's atmosphere?

2. What is the volume of sea-water required to raise sea-level by 20 feet equivalent to, according to Schmitt?

3. How much more heat energy must be imparted into the ice caps to raise sea levels catastrophically, according to Schmitt?

There is considerable debate over whether the "greenhouse gas" effect will raise the temperature of the atmosphere by between 1–5°C over the next 100 years. But even if you grant for the sake of argument the Warmist claim that the earth's atmosphere will go up a full five degrees Centigrade in temperature, [former Vice President] Al Gore's claim that ocean levels will rise 20 feet thanks to global warming seems to ignore the laws of thermodynamics. I am no climatologist, but I do know about physics.

Anyone who has ever spent time in a temperate climate following a snowy winter realizes that when the air temperature rises above 32°F the snow and ice do not melt immediately. We may experience many balmy early spring days with temperatures well above freezing while snow drifts slowly melt over days or weeks. Similarly, lakes and ponds take some time to freeze even days or weeks after the air temperature has plunged below zero. This is due to the latent heat of freezing/melting water, a physical concept long quantified in thermodynamics.

Climatologists Have Overlooked Basic Physics

That aspect of basic physics seems to have been overlooked by climatologists in their alarming claims of dramatic and rapid sea-level rise due to melting of the Antarctic ice caps and Greenland glaciers. But of course, we have learned that models predicting global warming also failed to take account of precipitation, so overlooking important factors ("inconvenient truths") should not cause much surprise anymore.

The scientific data necessary to calculate the amount of heat necessary to melt enough ice to raise ocean levels 20 feet is readily available on the internet, and the calculations needed to see if polar cap melting passes the laugh test are surprisingly simple. Nothing beyond multiplication and division, and because we will use metric measures for simplicity's sake, much of the multiplying is by ten or a factor of ten.

Let's review the math. The logic and calculations are within the grasp of anyone who cares to focus on the subject for minute or two, and speak for themselves.

I should first mention that the only source of energy to heat the atmosphere is the sun. The average energy per unit time (power) in the form of sunlight impinging on the earth is roughly constant year-to-year, and there are no means to increase or reduce the energy flux to the earth. The question merely is how much of this energy is trapped in the atmosphere and available to melt ice thus effecting "climate change".

Calculating Global Warming

How much heat must be trapped to raise the atmospheric temperature by a degree centigrade (or more) can be readily calculated, knowing the mass of the atmosphere and the specific heat of air. Specific heat is simply an empirically determined quantity that corresponds to the number of units of heat energy required to raise a specific mass of a substance, in this case air, by 1 degree in temperature. A common unit of energy familiar to most of us is the calorie. But for simplicity, in this calculation I will use the MKS [meter-kilogram-second] metric unit of the Joule (J), which, while perhaps unfamiliar to many readers in itself, is the numerator in the definition of our common unit of power, the Watt = Joule/second. . . .

We also know that [the mass of the atmosphere] is principally composed of air, so without loss of accuracy in what is essentially an "order of magnitude" calculation, it is fair to employ the specific heat of air at constant pressure, C_p. . . .

The Antarctic Ice Sheet Is Thickening

So, don't sell the beachfront property just yet—the jury seems as if it will be out a tad bit longer on global sea level rise since the precise cause of a rise is questionable. Testimonials by climate change alarmists that coastal regions of the world will be inundated as glacial melt water streams into the world's oceans have just been met with evidence that a large portion of the Antarctic ice sheet has thickened over the last of the 20th century. Evidence is scant that this observed sea level lowering from Anarctica won't continue long into the future.

"Sea Level Rise? Not From Antarctica Melting," World Climate Report, *December 5, 2006. www.worldclimatereport.com.*

While this has a value that changes with temperature, it doesn't change by orders of magnitude, consequently, I choose the value at 0°C, which, as we all know, is near to the global mean temperature at sea level. In this I err on the side of caution, overestimating the heat energy in the calculation below, because as we all know, both air pressure and temperature drop with altitude. I use the tilda ($\sim$) as symbol for "circa" or "approximately".

Mass of atmosphere: 5 x 10^{18}kg

Specific heat of air: 1.005 kJ/kg-°C

Heat needed to raise the temp of the atmosphere 1°C: $\sim$5 x 10^{18}kJ

Heat needed to raise the temp of the atmosphere 5°C: $\sim$2.5 x 10^{19}kJ

Will Melting Ice Raise Sea Levels?

It is instructive now to compare this quantity of heat with the amount that would be required to melt sufficient volume of ice from the Antarctic ice to raise the sea-level by 20 feet as predicted by Al Gore. Although ice floats, ice and water are very close in density, so at first approximation, it is fair to say that the volume of sea-water required to raise sea-level by 20 feet would be equivalent to the volume of ice that would need to melt to fill the ocean basins in order to cause that rise. Consequently, let's first roughly calculate the volume of seawater necessary.

The surface area of the earth ... 5.1×10^8 square kilometers, which I convert to 5.1×10^{14} square meters below for the purpose of our calculation. Al Gore's 20-foot-rise is equal to ~6 meter. Let's use the commonly cited figure that 70% of the earth's surface is covered by the oceans and seas. Accordingly,

Area of earth's surface: 5.1×10^{14} m^2

Proportion of earth's surface covered by water: 70%

Area of oceans and seas: ~3.6×10^{14} m^2

Sea level rise predicted by Al Gore: 20 feet = 6 m

Volume of water necessary to raise sea-level 20 feet: ~22×10^{15} m^3

Volume of ice that needs to melt to raise sea-level 20 feet: ~22×10^{15} m^3

Facts About Ice Melting

This is where the latent heat of melting comes into the equation. As we all know, when we drop an ice cube into our glass of water, soft-drink or adult-beverage, it quickly cools the drink. Heat is transferred to the ice from the liquid in order to melt the ice; this loss of heat cools and reduces the temperature of the liquid. This cooling continues until the ice melts completely.

Scientists have long known that a mixture of ice and water (ice-water) remains at the freezing/melting point ($0°C = 32°F$). Adding heat does NOT change the temperature, it just melts more ice; withdrawing heat does NOT change the temperature, it just freezes more water. The temperature of ice-water will not rise until all the ice is melted; conversely, the temperature of ice-water will not fall until all the water is frozen. The heat that would have otherwise raised the ice temperature is somehow "stored" in the melt water—hence "latent heat".

As an aside, the transformation of the latent-heat of steam into work via steam-engines has had, and continues to have, vast industrial importance. The early systematic study of steam-engines in order to improve their performance, laid the groundwork for the science of thermodynamics, which undergirds essentially all of physics and chemistry.

Latent Heat and Melting

It turns out that latent heats of melting (and evaporation) are generally very large quantities when compared to the amount of heat necessary to change temperatures. Also, as usual in such analyses we normalize to units of mass. Since the density of water/ice is roughly a thousand times higher than air, this also greatly impacts the magnitudes of energy involved, as you will see below. So let's proceed with the calculation.

The latent heat of melting of water . . . is 334 kJ/kg of water. One of the benefits of the metric system is that $1 \text{ ml} = 1 \text{ cm}^3 = 1$ g of water; this "built in" conversion simplifies many engineering calculations. Remembering this fact, we do not need to look up the density of water. Converting this density, $1 g/cm^3$, to MKS units, yields density of water $= 1000 \text{ kg/m}^3$. We now have all our data for the rough calculation:

Volume of ice that needs to melt (from above): $\sim 22 \times 10^{15}$

Density of water and ice: 1000 kg/m³

Mass of ice that needs to melt: $\sim 22 \times 10^{18} kg$

Latent heat of melting for water 3.34 x 10^2 kJ/kg

Heat necessary to melt ice to achieve 20-foot sea-level rise $\sim$7.4 x 10^{21}kJ

Following this "back of the envelope" calculation, let's compare the two energy values:

Heat needed to raise the temp of the atmosphere 5°C: $\sim$2.5 x 10^{19}kJ

Heat necessary to melt ice to achieve 20-foot sea-level rise $\sim$7.4 x 10^{21}kJ

Sea Levels Will Not Rise Catastrophically

There is a difference of 30* between these two figures, by implication extending the time-horizon for sea-level rise from 100 to 3000 years at the earliest. This does NOT mean that ice caps have not melted in the distant past nor that ice-age glaciers have not grown to cover much of the northern hemisphere; it simply means that the time scales involved to move sufficient quantities of heat to effect such melting or freezing occur over what we scientists commonly call "geological" time scales, i.e. tens or hundreds of thousands of years.

Even if sufficient heat is trapped in the atmosphere to raise it the maximum value predicted by anthropogenic "global warming" alarmists (5°C) over the next 100 years, *thirty times more heat energy must be imparted into the ice-caps to melt sufficient ice to raise sea-levels the catastrophic levels prophesied by Al Gore.*

---

* Editor's note: a transposed decimal point led to an incorrect multiple used here when this article was first published. The energy required is nevertheless hundreds of times greater than evidently assumed by Al Gore.

"The current and projected rate and scope of climate change in the Arctic presents a whole new threat as it is occurring faster than any other phenomenon that indigenous people have observed."

Polar Indigenous Peoples Are Threatened by Climate Change

Timo Koiurova, Henna Tervo, and Adam Stepien

In the following viewpoint, the writers argue that Arctic indigenous peoples are seriously threatened by climate change. Melting sea ice and rising temperatures affect the way of life of Arctic indigenous peoples by making travel on ice dangerous, diminishing the species available for hunting, damaging water supplies, and affecting food storage, among other problems. Although indigenous peoples have adapted in the past, climate change is happening so rapidly that the maintenance of indigenous identity and the survival of these cultures may be jeopardized, according to the authors. Timo Koiurova, Henna Tervo, and Adam Stepien are researchers at the Northern Institute for Environmental and Minority Law, located in Finland.

As you read, consider the following questions:

1. Who are some of the indigenous peoples who live in the Arctic, according to the authors?

2. What percentage of Inuit, Saami and people of Chukotka hunt seal, do the authors report?

3. According to the authors, why is the option of relocation for indigenous peoples now limited?

Indigenous peoples are the most threatened residents of the Arctic region in the light of climate change. Their living is closely interlaced with nature, which makes them especially vulnerable. The Arctic environment is at a state of irreversible change. The consequences of climate change include general warming, changes in ice and sea level, coastal erosion and thawing permafrost. The impacts on the indigenous communities are vast: culture, society, health and harvesting activities are influenced as well as infrastructure, transport and the basis of economy.

The Arctic marine area plays an important role in the living of many indigenous groups (e.g. in terms of hunting, fishing and travelling). The changes occurring in the Arctic marine pose a new threat for the traditional usage of the sea. For example, disappearing sea ice affects many species that are dependent on ice cover (e.g. polar bear, seal and whale) which makes the hunting activities of indigenous people complicated while rapid weather changes, occurrence of thin ice and severe weather conditions can make hunting dangerous. The role of the changing Arctic marine environment can be best understood by presenting the overall picture of indigenous communities. Therefore, after the situation of Arctic indigenous peoples has shortly been introduced, the general impacts of climate change . . . will be discussed in greater detail. The challenge that will be examined at the end is to find effective ways to support Arctic indigenous peoples to adapt to the consequences of climate change.

The Indigenous Peoples of the Arctic

Out of the total population of 4 million residents in the Arctic approximately 10% are indigenous.

Indigenous people in the Arctic belong to various groups (e.g. Inupiat, Yup'ik and Aleut in Alaska, Inuit in Greenland and Canada, Saami in Fennoscandia and Chukchi, Even, Evenk and Nenets in Russia) and there is a great variation of cultural, historical and economic backgrounds among them. The Arctic marine area plays a substantial role for many of the indigenous peoples. According to a recent study, out of the Inuit, Saami and people of Chukotka as many as 74% perform fishing, 31% hunt sea mammals, 21% hunt walrus and 42% hunt seal or ugruk.

Climate change is not the only cause of change in the Arctic. Most of the indigenous groups in the region have already undergone significant changes due to the globalization of the western way of life, state policies, modern transport and the introduction of mixed economic systems. It is important to note that these factors often occur simultaneously with climate change and in some cases it is difficult to separate the consequences of climate change from the other elements.

Indigenous peoples have traditionally been adaptive and resilient to change. However, the current and projected rate and scope of climate change in the Arctic presents a whole new threat as it is occurring faster than any other phenomenon that indigenous people have observed. Furthermore, the adaptive capacity of the indigenous peoples has altered as they are often more dependent on the outside world than in the past. The great variety of the legal, political, cultural and economic diversity among the Arctic countries influences the ability of the communities to cope with the changing environment.

The Negative Impact of Climate Change

Climate change is impacting on Inuit culture. Travel over regions of shifting ice is fraught with greater risk, making access to traditional food sources more difficult. Inuit, who are dependent on seasonal migrations of caribou, have reported not encountering the tundra foragers when expected.

Some coastal villages are exposed to the seas by the lack of ice. The village of Tuktoyaktuk is situated on the shores of the Beaufort Sea. Its beautiful location is now vulnerable to the ravages of coastal erosion.

The health of people in the Arctic is more and more susceptible to the climate changes. Longer exposure to sunlight and UV radiation can lead to an increased incidence of sunburn, skin cancer, immune-suppression-related disorders such as stress, and the introduction of new diseases to the Arctic by pests such as mosquitoes.

Kim Peterson,
"Arctic Climate Change," The Dominion,
December 19, 2004. www.dominion.ca.

The Impacts of Climate Change on Indigenous Communities

Climate change impacts on indigenous communities in a variety of ways. . . . Climate change causes and is projected to cause further changes in ice and snow conditions, waters' temperatures rise, permafrost thawing, coastal erosion, rising sea level and general warming. These consequences of climate change have an impact on indigenous harvesting activities, availability of resources, economy, society, culture and health. This is due to strong interrelation between indigenous cultures and environment inhabited by these groups. Additionally, housing, infrastructure and transport connections of coastal indigenous communities are seriously affected with rising maintenance costs and sometimes even the necessity of relocation.

How Will Indigenous Peoples Adapt to Climate Change?

In light of the most recent discoveries on climate change impacts, it appears that present means of adaptation are insufficient. The following suggests ways which could support indigenous peoples to adapt to the consequences of climate change.

New governance structures, devolution of legislative powers, new arrangements on land and natural resources management, adjustment of the existing national laws (e.g. regulating traditional harvesting to adjust better to the changing climate conditions). These are important solutions to be further developed at a national level. Empowerment of indigenous groups together with taking into account specific indigenous perspective forms the basis for successful adaptation.

International legal instruments. Several international treaties aimed at protecting the indigenous peoples' rights have already been adopted. Also, the awareness of a link between human rights and climate change is increasingly recognized. An indication of this development is a petition to IACHR [Inter-American Commission on Human Rights], filed by the Inuit, who claim that US climate policy violates their human rights. Even if the attempt eventually may prove unsuccessful, it may have other positive effects such as strengthening the position of indigenous peoples in general by attracting the attention of international community, media and the public.

Traditional measures. Some traditional mitigation and adaptation measures may still be applied (e.g. changes to harvesting methods and timing, adjusting cultural features to new conditions). However, indigenous cultures have undergone significant changes and some traditional means of adaptation are no longer available. Foremost relocation, which might have been a feasible option some decades ago, is presently limited by permanent settlement, development of elaborate infrastructure and lack of financial resources.

Modern technology and information. The use of modern technologies together with providing more precise weather and health information may prove valuable. Various forms of state support for communities. . .would be highly useful for climate change adaptation if directed towards the improvement of living conditions and the preservation of hunting culture in changing environment.

New branches of industry and trade. Indigenous economies are likely to be further supplemented by formal economic activities, such as tourism or resource extraction (although the cooperation with non-indigenous governmental or business actors is often required). This brings business and new jobs into the region. On the other hand, environment and indigenous identity may be in this way endangered. Finding balance between these aspects is probably the greatest challenge for indigenous sustainable development in the Arctic.

Eventually, since climate change is a continuous process that has various effects on different areas, adaptation measures need to be tailored for specific local conditions and adjusted to continuously altering conditions.

> *"Arctic communities have a long history of adaptation to extreme environments, to environmental changes . . . forced re-settlement and rapid cultural change."*

Polar Indigenous Peoples Have Adapted to Climate Change in the Past

Mirjam Macchi

In the following viewpoint, Mirjam Macchi argues that the polar regions are the places where the impacts of climate change are the most obvious. She contends that the extreme Arctic climate has always challenged indigenous peoples to survive, and they have developed a range of adaptive strategies as a result. Arctic indigenous peoples have valuable climate observation capabilities, based on their traditional knowledge, according to the writer. Partnerships among indigenous peoples and scientists will provide good coping strategies for the survival of Arctic cultures. Macchi is a writer and researcher for the International Union for Conservation of Nature.

Mirjam Macchi, "Oceans, Coastal Areas and Islands and Climate Change," *Indigenous and Traditional Peoples and Climate Change*, March 2008. Reproduced by permission.

107

As you read, consider the following questions:

1. How much did the air temperature increase in the Arctic in the twentieth century, according to Macchi?

2. According to the author, what are some of the ways that indigenous Arctic people have recognized political power?

3. What 2004 report benefited from the input of traditional people and how did it benefit, according to Macchi?

The Arctic and the Antarctic are the places on Earth where the impacts of climate change are the most obvious. The Arctic has experienced a warming trend in air temperature of as much as 5°C during the 20th century, and sees a continuous decrease in sea-ice extent. Further warming and increases in precipitation are projected for the 21st century. Predicted impacts of warming include: increased melting on Arctic glaciers and the Greenland ice sheet, which will retreat and thin close to their margins; substantial loss of sea ice and the opening of new sea routes; increased biological production; changes in species compositions on land and in the sea, poleward shifts in species assemblages and loss of some polar species. Changes in sea ice will alter the seasonal distributions, geographic ranges, patterns of migration, nutritional status, reproductive success, and ultimately the abundance and balance of species. . . .

Climate Change Will Impact Arctic Indigenous Peoples

These changes will have major impacts on human communities in the Arctic, and in particular indigenous peoples, whose longstanding traditions and ways of life could be threatened. . . .

The risks posed by climate change to traditional communities are probably best documented for the indigenous peoples of the Arctic. . . .

A few reasons can explain this: firstly, the extreme and unique climate of the Arctic makes it special enough to attract attention and trigger research on human adaptation capacities. The Arctic is also particularly sensitive to climate changes, which are more pronounced there than in any other region of the world. Finally, indigenous peoples have a recognized political power in the region, as they are for instance represented in the Arctic Council—a high-level forum for cooperation, coordination and interaction between Arctic States (USA, Canada, Denmark/Greenland, Iceland, Norway, Sweden, Finland and Russia) and indigenous communities.

It is recognized that the Arctic is now experiencing some of the most rapid and severe climate change on earth, and that changes will continue at an accelerated pace. This will have major physical, ecological, social, cultural and economic impacts, and might even jeopardize the survival of some traditional cultures.

Challenges and Opportunities

Shifts of vegetation zones, changes in animal species diversity, range and distribution, reduction of the extent and thickness of sea-ice, sea-level rise or increasing exposure to storm are some of the challenges that Arctic communities will have to face. While it is believed that most of the changes will have negative consequences for indigenous communities, these changes will open up new opportunities as well. They include expansion of marine shipping, increase in tourism and access to offshore oil and gas (though these so-called opportunities have their own environmental and social risks), enhanced marine fisheries, agriculture and forestry.

Arctic communities have a long history of adaptation to extreme environments, to environmental changes as well as to

Adaptive Capacity of the Inuit

It is sometimes asserted by Inuit leaders that their communities are and have been adaptable for centuries and thus that outsiders should not make culture-laden presumptions with respect to the (in)capacity of the Inuit to adapt. . . . [A]daptation by Inuit communities over the past two hundred can perhaps be characterized as a series of Inuit responses to imposed changes brought about by outsiders. The Inuit themselves have not participated in managing the sources of change. In this respect climate change has been no exception. . . . The Inuit are now seeking to go beyond responding to imposed change so as to participate in the design of regional, national and global strategies to manage the sources of climate change within our ken. This is the effort to create an "adaptation dialogue". For the Inuit to seek an adaptation dialogue gives rise to a number of questions: How can the adaptive capacity of the Inuit people and their forms of governance become part of the management of climate change? How can traditional environmental knowledge inform adaptation strategies?. . . What can be learned from past Inuit adaptations when facing adaptation to climate?

"Inuit Governance of Adaptation to Climate Change,"
Indigenous Peoples and Government, *2006. www.pag-ipg.com.*

other type of changes such as colonization, forced resettlement and rapid cultural change. While they have so far proved to be able to cope with those changes, it is recognized that climate change poses unprecedented challenges, and the question whether some indigenous peoples will be able to adapt is raised.

Examples of Indigenous Adaptations

While it is difficult to find any systematic study of Arctic indigenous communities' modern adaptation strategies to changing climates, some examples include:

Housing

- Shorelines reinforcement and moving buildings from the shoreline, due to soil erosion caused by decreasing permafrost

- Use of innovative building material to support structures, due to ground instability caused by changing permafrost patterns

Subsistence

- Increased water quality testing and consumption of bottled water due decreasing water quality and accessibility

- Changing hunting habits, by either hunting with boats or switching to fishing as well as hunting quotas

- Increased consumption of store-bought foods due to scarcer local foods

Emergency preparedness

- Extension of danger zones in avalanche prone areas and expansion of research and rescue teams due to increased snow slides and avalanches

- Development of better emergency preparedness plans by having more supplies during travel or avoiding travel during periods of bad weather

- Increasing use of Global Positioning Systems (GPS), cellular phones and CB radio. . .

[A]daptations come in a huge variety of forms. They include spontaneous and planned (both reactive or anticipatory) adaptations, short or long term, localized or widespread, etc. The few examples above represent indeed a mixture of responses, from increased preparedness against natural hazards, accommodation of traditional ways of life (housing or hunting, for instance) to actual shifts toward less traditional ways of life, which could indicate the beginning of a possible loss of traditional cultures.

The Value of Traditional Knowledge

The value of traditional knowledge and observations made by indigenous people on climate change has been clearly recognized in the Arctic. The Arctic Climate Impact Assessment (ACIA) report, a four-year study of Arctic climate released in November 2004, benefited from the input of traditional people. It further recognizes that traditional knowledge provides a good supplement to and enrichment of scientific data. One of the authors of the report, [J. Couzin] cited by *Science* said that "The [ACIA] report was very instrumental in awakening people to the value of traditional knowledge as 'very solid science'". The partnership between traditional peoples and scientists is also meant to make science useful to local peoples, and give them another perspective on the changes that are taking place in the Arctic.

This type of collaboration with indigenous communities seems however more focused on improving understanding of physical and ecological impacts of climate change in the Arctic than social and cultural impacts. It will be equally important to include indigenous peoples at the decision-making level, so that their experience and successful adaptation strategies can help shape new forms of governance and livelihoods to meet the challenge of climate change.

> *"Above all other factors contributing to the need to list polar bears as threatened, however, is the unequivocal and extensive loss of polar bear habitat due to global warming.*

Polar Bears Are Endangered by Climate Change

Jamie Rappaport Clark

In the following viewpoint, excerpted from testimony to the U.S. House of Representatives, Jamie Rappaport Clark argues that polar bears are a threatened species. According to Clark, global warming is melting sea ice, thus destroying polar bear habitat and hunting territory. She further argues that oil and gas development in the Arctic will endanger the polar bears through pollution and through increased greenhouse gases caused by carbon-based fuels. Clark is executive vice president of Defenders of Wildlife, a conservation and environmental advocacy organization headquartered in Washington, D.C.

As you read, consider the following questions:

1. What body of water does Clark want to protect from new oil and gas leasing?

Jamie Rappaport Clark, "Testimony before the Select Committee on Energy Independence and Global Warming, On Thin Ice: The Future of the Polar Bear," United States House of Representatives, January 17, 2008. Reproduced by permission of the author.

2. What did 2007 satellite images reveal about the state of the Arctic ice cover, according to Clark?

3. How much of the polar bear's core habitat does the Minerals Management Service (MMS) want to open to gas and oil development, according to Clark?

The Arctic has become "ground zero" for the most visible adverse early effects of global warming, a place where dramatic coastal erosion threatens human communities and where the accelerating disappearance of sea ice has become emblematic of the underlying problems directly attributable to our society's destructive dependence on carbon-based fossil fuels. Polar bears are the most visible, and most poignant, symbol of the devastating impact global warming is already having on wildlife. It is no accident that the world's leading soft drink seller, Coca-Cola, has adopted polar bears as a marketing image. People respond to these magnificent creatures. Thus, as reports of melting Arctic sea ice proliferate and images of polar bears starving or drowning find their way into the public consciousness, polar bears are awakening us all to the threat from global warming. Or almost all of us.

Unfortunately, there is still ongoing denial by the [George W.] Bush administration [2000–2008]. By continuing to delay listing polar bears as threatened, and at the same time pushing forward new oil and gas leases in essential polar bear habitat, the Bush administration is continuing its outrageous pattern of denial and foot-dragging in response to global warming, while actually promoting the burning of fossil fuels that will only make the problem worse—for wildlife and humans. . . .

Polar Bears Must Be Protected

[I]t is past time for this administration to list polar bears as a threatened species, to follow the requirements of the Endangered Species Act and carefully review proposed oil and gas leases and other federal actions to ensure that they will not jeopardize the continued existence of polar bears, and to refrain from any new oil and gas leasing in the Chukchi Sea and other polar bear habitat until adequate measures are in place to prevent harm from such activity to polar bears and their habitat. If the administration will finally show responsible leadership, the polar bear can serve not just as a symbol of the harmful impacts of global warming, but as a beacon of hope for helping all wildlife survive global warming. . . .

[T]here are numerous factors that support listing polar bears as threatened. These include the continued hunting of polar bears and international trade in polar bear parts, potential for increased vulnerability to disease and parasites resulting from habitat shifts due to global warming, increased exposure to human-caused disturbance and pollution, and the inadequacy of existing regulatory mechanisms to respond to the threat from global warming. Above all other factors contributing to the need to list polar bears as threatened, however, is the unequivocal and extensive loss of polar bear habitat due to global warming.

The Arctic Sea Ice Is Melting Away

The Arctic sea ice which provides habitat for polar bears is literally melting away. Research conducted by experts at the U.S. National Snow and Ice Data Center in Colorado shows that for the second year in a row Arctic sea ice has failed to reform after the summer melt. Last September [2007], satellite images showed Arctic ice cover to be at its lowest extent since monitoring began in 1978, a reduction of 8.7 percent per decade. Scientists confirmed that summer sea ice retreated even more during summer 2007.

The extent of sea ice on the Arctic Ocean, of course, fluctuates with the season. The ice melts during the six months of daylight, reaching its minimum point in September. Normally, during the winter, sea ice forms to compensate for what was lost over the summer, but last winter the Arctic experienced warmer than usual temperatures preventing ice from forming and causing the ice that did form to be thinner. Reduction of the extent of sea ice in both the winter and summer is an indicator that the Arctic is experiencing a positive feedback effect, whereby warmer temperatures melt sea ice, causing more open water that absorbs sunlight, which, in turn, causes more ice to melt. In addition, emissions of black carbon, or soot, also may be accelerating the melting of sea ice by reducing its reflectivity. If this cycle continues as predicted, models indicate that there will be no sea ice left by 2070, or earlier. Already parts of the Arctic Ocean remain ice-free year round, such as a large area in the Barents Sea, home to an estimated 2,000–5,000 polar bears.

The Loss of Sea Ice Kills Polar Bears

Loss of sea ice results in dire consequences for polar bears. Sea ice provides a platform from which polar bears hunt for ringed seals and other prey. As seals follow the receding sea ice, they may be too far from land for polar bears to reach them. Polar bears, though good swimmers over short distances, are not able to traverse large open expanses of water. In 2004, MMS [Minerals Management Service, a division of the U.S. Department of Interior] found four bears that had drowned off the northern coast of Alaska where the ice cap had retreated 160 miles north of land. Unable to reach the sea ice, polar bears that remain on land will likely come into conflict with humans, leading to killing of so-called nuisance bears.

In particular, lack of sea ice will have a negative impact on female bears. MMS has found that, in the last ten years, 60 percent of female polar bears were denning on land and 40 percent were denning on ice, where previously the percentages were reversed. Polar bears that den on land have more difficulty traveling between land and ice, forcing them to leave the ice and stop hunting earlier before the ice has retreated too far for them to find their preferred denning areas on land. Less and thinner ice may also disrupt the rearing of polar bear cubs for those populations that den on the ice.

Polar Bears Will Be Extinct in Alaska

Here is the most dire warning of all: Reductions in Arctic sea ice and increases in the rate at which Arctic sea ice is disappearing led the U.S. Geological Survey to conclude that U.S. populations of polar bears will be extirpated [made extinct] by 2050. The government's own scientists predict that, if we continue with business as usual in emitting greenhouse gas pollution, by mid-century, polar bears will no longer exist in Alaska. *Case closed.* Polar bears must be listed as threatened under the Endangered Species Act. In addition, immediate steps must be taken to halt their downward spiral. These include refraining from oil and gas leasing in the Chukchi Sea and changing our energy policy to reduce greenhouse gas pollution. If we act now, there is hope for polar bears, the Arctic ecosystem, and ourselves and our children. . . .

Oil and Gas Leasing Will Harm Polar Bears

The potential for harm to polar bears from oil and gas leasing in the Chukchi Sea is substantial. MMS is proposing to open nearly 30 million acres of core habitat critical to the survival of polar bears to oil and gas development. Such development is highly risky and detrimental to polar bears and other Arctic wildlife. Oil and gas development routinely produces massive air pollution emissions, including increased emissions of greenhouse gases that cause global warming. The sensitive Arctic marine environment is subject to serious damage, from activities ranging from seismic survey blasts to routine toxic discharges of spent drill muds, borehole cuttings, and wastewater, dumped directly into one of the most pristine and biologically sensitive marine environments on the planet. The risk of damage from oil spills, leaks, fires, and other accidents, exacerbated by an industry history of lax oversight and enforcement, poses a serious threat to Arctic wildlife.

Most disturbing of all, no technology presently exists that can even begin to successfully clean up spilled oil at sea in the meteorological and sea-state conditions prevalent in the Arctic. Furthermore, no oil spill technology currently exists to adequately respond to a spill in broken-sea-ice conditions such as those prevailing in the Chukchi Sea. Once an oil spill moves under the ice sheet, which is essential to the breeding, feeding, and sheltering of polar bears and the entire Arctic marine life community, there is no way to even track its movements. Oil will not biodegrade but will remain highly toxic for up to a century or more, continually leaking out at unpredictable intervals to poison our wildlife and foul delicate lagoons and hundreds of miles of inaccessible shorelines. For polar bears, as well as the resident walrus and shorebird populations, and for the migrating bowhead and beluga whales in the Chukchi Sea, the consequences are unthinkable.

The Use of Fossil Fuels Must Be Reduced

In addition to the potential for direct harm to polar bears and their habitat from oil and gas development in the Chukchi Sea and elsewhere, there is the indirect, but equally devastating, impact of promoting additional burning of fossil fuels, which increases greenhouse gas pollution that causes global warming. We have reached a point . . . , where we cannot continue business as usual. We cannot continue to promote the burning of fossil fuels if we are going to stabilize atmospheric greenhouse gas concentrations and stop human-caused global warming. The plight of polar bears is a warning to us that we must act now to reduce our use of fossil fuels and consequent production of greenhouse gas pollution.

This is so much bigger than a singular focus on the polar bear, regardless of the importance of this species itself. Given what we now clearly know about the drastic implications of

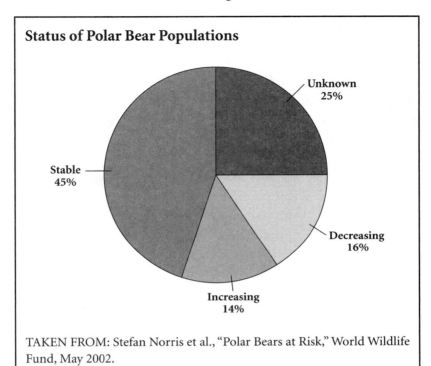

Status of Polar Bear Populations

Unknown
25%

Stable
45%

Decreasing
16%

Increasing
14%

TAKEN FROM: Stefan Norris et al., "Polar Bears at Risk," World Wildlife Fund, May 2002.

global warming for human society worldwide, it is clear that the [George W. Bush] administration's stumbling approach to making these decisions concerning the polar bear and the Chukchi Sea are emblematic of something bigger and very troubling. Even with all the evidence out there on the seriousness of global warming, this administration still—incomprehensibly—refuses to believe it. Or, they do believe it and yet still will not take responsible action because of their commitment to serve private and political interests that are not in the best interests of the country or the future. Either way, it is a poor reflection on this administration and the American people are ill-served by it.

Crossroads for the Polar Bear

In conclusion, . . . we have come to a crossroads—for the polar bear, for all life in the Arctic seas, and for our own global

climate future. It is long past time to begin seriously addressing global warming. The Bush administration should move
forward immediately to list the polar bear as a threatened species and to fully comply with the requirements of the Endangered Species Act. The administration should also withdraw
the proposed oil and gas leases in the Chukchi Sea, while it
fully complies with the consultation requirements of the Endangered Species Act. The administration should also refrain
from any further oil and gas leasing in the Chukchi Sea or
other polar bear habitat until adequate measures are in place
to protect polar bears and their habitat from the harmful effects of such development. Most importantly, this administration or, more likely, the next one, should work with the Congress to develop an energy policy that will reduce our use of
fossil fuels, our production of greenhouse gas pollution, and
that will protect polar bears, other imperiled wildlife, and, ultimately, ourselves and future generations from the harmful
impacts of global warming.

> *"By and large, the [National Center for Policy Analysis] study finds that polar bear populations are in good shape."*

Polar Bears Are Not Endangered By Climate Change

H. Sterling Burnett

In the following viewpoint, H. Sterling Burnett argues that there is no basis in the claim that global warming is endangering polar bear populations. He first refutes that the climate of the Arctic is warming. Next, he provides evidence that the polar ice cover is thickening, not melting. Further, he argues that polar bear populations are not in trouble, but rather are adapting successfully to changing conditions. Burnett is a senior fellow with the National Center for Policy Analysis.

As you read, consider the following questions:

1. In what year during the twentieth century was the Arctic's maximum air temperature recorded, according to a Russian study cited by Burnett?

2. In addition to seals, what do polar bears eat, according to Burnett?

3. According to Burnett, are polar bear populations declining or increasing in areas that show air temperature decreases?

Recently, some scientists have claimed that human-caused global warming poses a significant threat to the survival of many species. For most species at risk, they argue, warming will cause the range of suitable habitat to shift faster than either the species (or their food sources) can move or adapt to a new range. For other species, they say, suitable habitat will cease to exist altogether. Among the species claimed to be at high risk of extinction from human-caused global warming is the charismatic polar bear.

Indeed, in February 2005 the Center for Biological Diversity filed a petition with the United States Fish and Wildlife Service [USFWS] to list the polar bear as endangered or threatened. The petition was later joined by the Natural Resources Defense Council and Greenpeace. In response, the USFWS initiated a formal status review to determine if the polar bear should be protected throughout its range.

A new NCPA [National Center for Policy Analysis] study by Dr. David Legates, director of the University of Delaware's Center for Climatic Research and state climatologist, examines the claim that global warming threatens to cause polar bear extinction and finds little basis for fear. By and large, the study finds that polar bear populations are in good shape.

Is the Arctic Warming?

In the study, *Climate Science: Climate Change and Its Impacts*, Legates reviewed the claims that global warming is causing an unnatural increase in Arctic temperatures, posing a threat to the thickness and extent of sea ice and thus to the polar bears who rely upon it. In particular, he examined assertions made in the 2004 *Arctic Climate Impact Assessment* (hereafter, the *Arctic Assessment*), an international project of the Arctic Council and the International Arctic Science Committee (IASC).

Legates finds that their claims of an impending, human-induced Arctic meltdown are not supported by the evidence. For example, the *Arctic Assessment* proclaimed that Arctic air temperature trends provide an early and strong indication that global warming is causing polar ice caps and glaciers to melt. However, current research suggests that coastal stations in Greenland are instead experiencing a cooling trend, and average summer air temperatures at the summit of the Greenland Ice Sheet have decreased at the rate of 4°F per decade since measurements began in 1987.

In addition, the *Arctic Assessment* ignored a relatively recent long-term analysis of records from coastal stations in Russia. Russian coastal-station records of both the extent of sea ice and the thickness of fast ice (ice fixed to the shoreline or seafloor) extending back 125 years show significant variability over 60- to 80-year periods. Moreover, the maximum air temperature reported for the 20th century was in 1938, when it was nearly 0.4°F warmer than in 2000. The Russian study concludes that actual temperature measurements do not show the increased warming predicted by computer climate models.

However, even if warming is occurring, it has happened before, as ice cores from Baffin Island and sea core sediments from the Chukchi Sea show. For example, in Alaska, the onset of a warming in 1976–1977 ended the multi-decade cold trend in the mid-20th century and simply returned temperatures to those experienced in the early 20th century. Sharp, substantial fluctuations are typical of the historic pattern of natural climate variability extending back several centuries. And, as expected in response to natural variability, Alaskan ecosystems have responded rapidly and visibly to this recent warmth. By contrast, if the recent warmth were human-induced by constant additions of greenhouse gases to the atmosphere, responses in the Arctic region would be expected to be gradual and modest when viewed within any short time period.

Is Warming Causing Sea Ice to Melt?

According to the *Arctic Assessment*, human-caused warming in the Arctic will necessarily lead to decreased sea ice thickness and extent. However, air temperature is only one factor that influences sea ice; the frequency and velocity of the wind also has an effect. When the Arctic is relatively calm, it is easier for sea ice to develop. During stormy periods, surface winds churn the water and move existing ice, making it more difficult for sea ice to form.

A study commissioned by Canada's Department of Fisheries and Oceans examined the relationship between air temperature and sea ice and concluded, "the possible impact of global warming appears to play a minor role in changes to Arctic sea ice." Rather, the Canadian study found that changing wind patterns are the primary cause of changing sea ice distributions. Moreover, while sea ice has decreased in the Arctic, it has remained relatively constant (or even increased slightly) in the Antarctic since 1978.

Is Global Warming Killing Polar Bears?

The *Arctic Assessment* concludes, "global warming could cause polar bears to go extinct by the end of the century by eroding the sea ice that sustains them." According to the assessment, the threat to polar bears is threefold: changes in rainfall or snowfall amounts or patterns could affect the ability of seals, the bears' primary prey, to successfully reproduce and raise their pups; decreased sea ice could result in a greater number of polar bears drowning or living more on land, negatively affecting their diet (forcing them to rely on their fat stores prior to hibernation); and unusual warm spells could cause the collapse of winter dens or force more bears into less-desirable denning areas.

Though polar bears are uniquely adapted to the Arctic region, they are not wedded solely to its coldest parts nor are they restricted to a specific Arctic diet. Aside from a variety of seals, they eat fish, kelp, caribou, ducks, sea birds and scavenged whale and walrus carcasses. In addition, as discussed above, Arctic air temperatures were as high as present temperatures in the 1930s and polar bears survived.

Interestingly, the World Wildlife Fund (WWF), an international organization that has worked for 50 years to protect endangered species, has also written on the threats posed to polar bears from global warming. However, their own research seems to undermine their fears. According to the WWF, about 20 distinct polar bear populations exist, accounting for approximately 22,000 polar bears worldwide. As the figure shows, population patterns do not show a temperature-linked decline:

- Only two of the distinct population groups, accounting for about 16.4 percent of the total population, are decreasing.

- Ten populations, approximately 45.4 percent of the total number, are stable.

- Another two populations—about 13.6 percent of the total number of polar bears—are increasing.

The status of the remaining six populations (whether they are stable, increasing or decreasing in size) is unknown.

Moreover, when the WWF report is compared with the Arctic air temperature trend studies discussed earlier, there is a strong positive (instead of negative) correlation between air temperature and polar bear populations. Polar bear populations are declining in regions (like Baffin Bay) that have experienced a decrease in air temperature, while areas where polar bear populations are increasing (near the Bering Strait and the Chukchi Sea) are associated with increasing air temperatures. Thus it is difficult to argue that rising air temperatures will necessarily and directly lead to a decrease in polar bear populations.

Are human activities causing a warming in the Arctic, affecting the sea ice extent, longevity and thickness? Contradictory data exists. What seems clear is that polar bears have survived for thousands of years, including both colder and warmer periods. There may be threats to the future survival of the polar bear, but global warming is not primary among them.

Periodical Bibliography

The following articles have been selected to supplement the diverse views presented in this chapter.

Scott G. Borgerson — "Arctic Meltdown: The Economic and Security Implications of Global Warming," *Foreign Affairs*, March-April 2008.

Elizabeth Gossman — "The Big Melt: Notes from the Front Lines of Climate Change, *Earth Island Journal*, vol. 23, no. 2, Summer 2008.

International Polar Foundation — "Indigenous Communities and Climate Change: A New Challenge for Adaptation," May 24, 2007. www.sciencepoles.org.

MPA News — "Before the Ice Melts: Experts Discuss Proactive Protection of the Arctic Ocean in Anticipation of Climate Change," vol. 9, no. 2, August 2007.

Volker Mrasek — "Point of No Return for the Arctic Climate?" *Speigel Online*, December 4, 2008. www.spiegel.de.

Terry O'Neill — "The Bear Facts: Canada's Inuit Say the Polar Bear Isn't Threatened by Global Warming or Hunting," *Western Standard*, vol. 4, no. 3, April 23, 2007.

Stephanie Renfrow — "Arctic Sea Ice Down to Second-Lowest Extent; Likely Record-Low Volume," National Snow and Ice Data Center, October 2, 2008.

Matthew Rusling — "Coast Guard Unprepared for Climate Change in the Arctic," *National Defense*, vol. 93, no. 657, August 2008.

Anna Salleh — "Antarctica DNA Gives Climate Coping Clues," *Australian Broadcasting Corporation News in Science*, October 14, 2008.

Science Centric — "Antarctic Fossils Reveal Much Warmer Continent," August 5, 2008. www.sciencecentric.com.

OPPOSING
VIEWPOINTS®
SERIES

CHAPTER 3

Should the Natural Resources of the Polar Regions Be Developed?

Chapter Preface

In 1990, the Scottish punk rock band Oi Polloi released the song "World Park Antarctica," on their album *In Defense of Our Earth*, as a plea to world governments to continue the protection of the Antarctic regions. While it is difficult to say whether this song had any effect on the nations that make up the Antarctic Treaty System (ATS) and who jointly make decisions concerning the Antarctic, the idea of a World Park is one that has had ongoing support from around the globe.

To place the idea of World Park Antarctica in context, it is necessary to go back to 1957–1958 International Geophysical Year. In that year, twelve countries conducted cooperative scientific research on the Antarctic continent. In a statement issued by U.S. President Dwight D. Eisenhower on May 3, 1958, he invited the eleven other countries to join with the United States to draft an Antarctic Treaty. Eisenhower announced in his statement:

> The United States is dedicated to the principle that the vast uninhabited wastes of Antarctica shall be used only for peaceful purposes. We do not want Antarctica to become an object of political conflict. . . . We propose that Antarctica shall be open to all nations to conduct scientific or other peaceful activities there. We also propose that joint administrative arrangements be worked out to ensure the successful accomplishment of these and other peaceful purposes.

Out of these meeting grew the ATS, which was signed and put into effect on June 23, 1961. Seven of the original signatories have land claims in Antarctica, including Argentina, Australia, Chile, France, New Zealand, Norway, and the United Kingdom. Other nations, including the United States, reserved the right to make territorial land claims. Since 1961, thirty-five additional countries have agreed to the Antarctic Treaty, and sixteen of these have demonstrated their interest in Antarctica by "conducting substantial research activity there," according to information on the ATS Summit 2009 Web site.

In 1975, according to Greenpeace, an environmental activist organization, New Zealand proposed that Antarctica should be named a "world park" and be governed in much the same way that national parks around the world are governed. This resolution did not pass, but many nations and environmental activists continued to believe that this was the best possible outcome for Antarctica. Then, in 1988, after years of international negotiations concerning mineral rights, a Special Antarctic Treaty Consultative Meeting held in New Zealand adopted the Antarctic Minerals Convention. Not all nations agreed to sign the Convention. According to the Australian Antarctic Division Web site, Australian Prime Minister Hawke "announced that Australia was opposed to mining in Antarctica and would not sign the Minerals Convention."

As a consequence, more negotiations were held, leading to what has become known as "The Madrid Protocol," a document that "provides that protection of the Antarctic environment . . . must be fundamental . . . in the planning and conduct of all human activities in Antarctica." This treaty entered into force on January 14, 1998. The Protocol prohibits mining for an indefinite period of time, but after fifty years, the ATS can review and modify this provision.

The Madrid Protocol, and its subsequent four annexes, thus in effect established World Park Antarctica, a protected place where science can be conducted and the environment will be protected. However, as climate change increases the possibility that mining could be accomplished more easily in Antarctica, there is fear among environmentalists that nations might once again decide that they should develop the resources of the continent without regard for environmental impacts.

Thus, while the idea of World Park Antarctica is one that nearly all nations of the world support philosophically, it remains to be seen whether they will continue to support the Madrid Protocol politically and economically. The writers of the following viewpoints are deeply divided concerning the development of resources in both Antarctica and the Arctic.

> *"We conclude that an immediate large-scale protection. . . of Arctic resources is warranted, and that the business as usual outlook in the mid- and long-term future will be devastating for. . . Arctic resources."*

The Natural Resources of the Arctic Should Be Protected

Falk Huettmann and Sue Hazlett

In the following viewpoint, Falk Huettmann and Sue Hazlett argue that before there is any widespread development of the Arctic, nations must come together to discuss how best to protect the irreplaceable resources of the region. They further assert that nations have not used management techniques in the Arctic that will ensure sustainability of resources. Data collected through their research, they contend, indicate that immediate protection is necessary as a strategy for "global survival." Huettmann and Hazlett are researchers with the Institute of Arctic Biology and the University of Alaska, respectively.

Falk Huettmann and Sue Hazlett, "Changing the Arctic: Adding Immediate Protection to the Equation," *International Polar Year*, October 21, 2008. Copyright © 2007-2008 International Polar Year. Reproduced by permission.

As you read, consider the following questions:

1. According to the authors, what three factors have piqued an interest in the Arctic not previously seen?

2. What has driven management decisions in the Arctic, according to the authors?

3. What do Huettmann and Hazlett state as their purpose?

The Arctic represents a region of the globe directly affected by climate change, human disturbance and natural variation. In addition to acting as the global weather machine, it is considered one of the last remaining "wilderness" areas. However, the warming of the Arctic, a prospect of an ice-free maritime route across the top of the world, and the International Polar Year (IPY), has piqued an interest in the Arctic not previously seen. Prospects of shipping routes, tourism, oil and gas development, and new commercial fisheries have started a land rush by various nations to claim a piece of the northern oceans. The Arctic is in danger of being given away piecemeal as each nation asserts claims and then rushes to develop or exploit their territory to aid in establishing ownership.

Haphazard Conservation Measures

A wider public discussion on the protection and management of this unique zone has not happened, and despite, or perhaps because of, globalization, protection is still difficult to implement. So far, if at all, only haphazard conservation measures have been considered. Most lack either focus, enforcement, or a performance review. The recent listing of polar bears in the US is a prime example, and Alaska is in the process of appealing the listing for fear protection will interfere with oil development and related transportation in the Alaskan Arctic. Other species in decline include the ivory gull, thick-billed murres, Kittlitz's murrelets, some eider duck species, various shorebirds, and Arctic cod. Many other crucial components of the Arctic biodiversity have not even been assessed, calling for the Precautionary Principle, as promoted by IUCN [International Union for Conservation of Nature]. Science-based adaptive management, a management method widely suggested to attain sustainability, has not been applied to the Arctic. . . . [W]e describe and assess the existing protection schema, and the pros and cons of increased protection in the Arctic, as well as how it links with global sustainability in monetary, biodiversity, and other terms. We are in a strong position to do this assessment because for the first time, we were able to assemble over 45 data sets in a consistent format and as GIS [geographic information systems] layers for the entire circumpolar Arctic.

Biodiversity, Indigenous Peoples, and the Environment Must Be Considered

So what would be the best level of protection for the Arctic and how would this be accomplished? With the Antarctic Treaty for instance, half of the Polar regions have basically been protected for decades. In contrast, few Arctic conservation zones exist, and they were virtually derived ad hoc, without any relevant principles of democratic governance and management practices. There has consistently been a history among nations of protecting 'rock and ice', and most current protected areas within the Arctic are of this type. If individual nations are each left to decide the level and area of protected areas, this concept would likely be the case for any future mandated protection. Many decisions were made without proper data and driven by specific agendas. Promotion of economic growth and nationalism have driven management decisions in the Arctic rather than a consideration of biodiversity, indigenous people and potential ecological services. As more development occurs, protection appears to continue to be an ad hoc process that would just protect an area with no per-

Protected Areas of the Arctic Regions, 2005

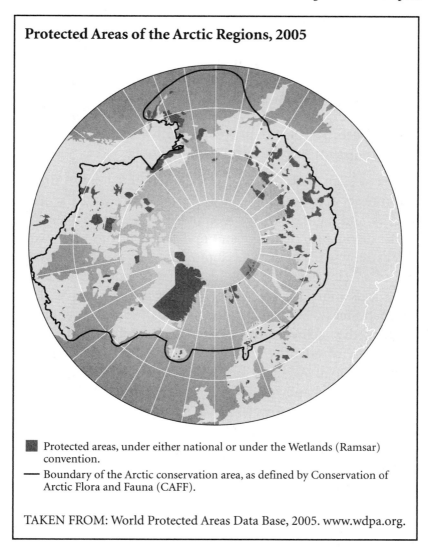

Protected areas, under either national or under the Wetlands (Ramsar) convention.

— Boundary of the Arctic conservation area, as defined by Conservation of Arctic Flora and Fauna (CAFF).

TAKEN FROM: World Protected Areas Data Base, 2005. www.wdpa.org.

ceived economic value. This is also true if protection is mandated to a certain percentage of the overall Arctic, or of each country's territory (the Rio Convention [The 1992 United Nations Declaration on Environment and Development] figure is a meager 10%). It is known from elsewhere that a small fragmented network of conservation features does not achieve well. [Our] purpose . . . is to put forth the concept of considering the Arctic as an entire ecosystem, take long-distance animal migration and energy flows into account, and propose the proper use of Strategic Conservation Planning to implement conservation plans on an international level before wholesale development of the Arctic begins. . . .

Immediate, Large Scale Protection Is Warranted

However, such tools are only a first step and require further fine-tuning, approval and use by various governments, stakeholders and legislation. We would highly welcome the wider public discussion, challenge and update of our modeling work. It is extremely likely that developing the Arctic will involve the loss of species, habitats, and sustainability detrimental to existing legislation. We are proposing that the real legacy of the International Polar Year is indeed a large protected circumpolar park that achieves the larger sustainability goals in the framework of adaptive management. Science-based adaptive management of Arctic resources can only be achieved when based on sound and mutually accepted data. Such a database, presented at a central web portal, still needs to be assembled and constantly be improved. It can only go hand-in-hand with high-quality monitoring efforts that feed into such efforts and link directly with policy.

We conclude that an immediate large-scale protection (e.g. over 30%) of Arctic resources is warranted, and that the business as usual outlook in the mid- and long-term future will be devastating for most national Arctic resources and destroying global resilience. Thus, adding protection to Arctic management is not only a best professional-practice, in full agreement with the original sprit of the conservation laws, or an ideology, but an inherent part of a global survival strategy.

VIEWPOINT *2*

| "*[Arctic] resources, especially the hydro-carbons, . . .have the potential to significantly enhance the economy and the energy security of North America and the world.*"

National Security Requires U.S. Development of the Arctic

Ariel Cohen, Lajos F. Szaszdi, and Jim Dolbow

In the following viewpoint, the authors argue that the Arctic is becoming strategically important to the United States. They further contend that the natural resources of the Arctic, particularly gas and oil, are necessary for the U.S. economy and energy security. They provide a series of steps the United States must take to protect its interests in the Arctic, including authorizing oil production in the Artic National Wildlife Refuge. Ariel Cohen is a senior research fellow and Ljos F. Szaszdi is a researcher at the Heritage Foundation, a conservative think tank in Washington, D.C. Jim Dolbow is a defense analyst at the U.S. Naval Institute.

Ariel Cohen, Lajos F. Szaszdi and Jim Dolbow, "The New Cold War: Reviving the U.S. Presence in the Arctic," *Heritage Foundation Backgrounder*, October 30, 2008. Copyright © 2008 The Heritage Foundation. Reproduced by permission.

As you read, consider the following questions:

1. According to the authors, how large is Russia's claim for Arctic Territory submitted to the United Nation's Convention on the Law of the Sea?

2. Why do the authors advise the United States to accelerate the acquisition of icebreakers?

3. In what ways do the authors believe the United States should play a leadership role in the Arctic?

The Arctic is quickly reemerging as a strategic area where vital U.S. interests are at stake. The geopolitical and geoeconomic importance of the Arctic region is rising rapidly, and its mineral wealth will likely transform the region into a booming economic frontier in the 21st century. The Arctic coasts and continental shelf are estimated to hold large deposits of oil, natural gas, methane hydrate (natural gas) clusters, and large quantities of valuable minerals.

With the shrinking of the polar ice cap, extended navigation through the Northwest Passage along the northern coast of North America may soon become possible with the help of icebreakers. Similarly, Russia is seeking to make the Northern Sea Route along the northern coast of Eurasia navigable for considerably longer periods of the year. Opening these shorter routes will significantly cut the time and costs of shipping.

Despite the Arctic's strategic location and vast resources, the U.S. has largely ignored this region. The United States needs to develop a comprehensive policy for the Arctic, including diplomatic, naval, military, and economic policy components. This should include swiftly mapping U.S. territorial claims to determine their extent and to defend against claims by other countries. With oil and gas prices recently at historic highs in a tight supply and demand environment, the rich hydrocarbon resources in the Arctic may bring some relief to consumers. These resources, especially the hydrocarbons, also have the potential to significantly enhance the economy and the energy security of North America and the world.

Russian Ambitions in the Arctic

Russia recognizes the multifaceted potential of the Arctic and is moving rapidly to assert its national interests. Moscow has submitted a claim to the U.N. [United Nations] Convention on the Law of the Sea to an area of 460,000 square miles—the size of Germany, France, and Italy combined. The Kremlin is pursuing its interests by projecting military power into the region and by using diplomatic instruments such as the Law of the Sea Treaty. Russia made a show of planting its flag on the Arctic seabed in August 2007 and has resumed strategic bomber flights over the Arctic for the first time since the end of the Cold War.

While paying lip service to international law, Russia's ambitious actions hearken back to 19th-century statecraft rather than the 21st-century law-based policy and appear to indicate that the Kremlin believes that credible displays of power will settle conflicting territorial claims. By comparison, the West's posture toward the Arctic has been irresolute and inadequate. This needs to change.

Reestablishing the U.S. Arctic Presence

The United States should not rely on the findings of other nations that are mapping the Arctic floor. Timely mapping results are necessary to defending and asserting U.S. rights in bilateral and multilateral fora [tribunal or court]. The U.S. needs to increase its efforts to map the floor of the Arctic Ocean to determine the extent of the U.S. Outer Continental Shelf (OCS) and ascertain the extent of legitimate U.S. claims to territory beyond its 200-nautical-mile exclusive economic zone. To accomplish this, the U.S. needs to upgrade its icebreaker fleet. The U.S. should also continue to cooperate and

U.S. and Russian Interests in the Arctic

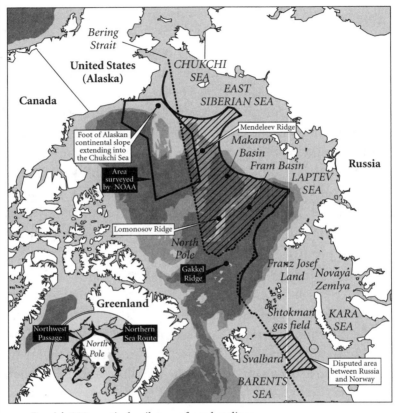

— Russia's 200-nautical-mile zone from baselines

···· Boundaries of Russia's claim filed in 2001

▱ Area of continental shelf beyond 200 miles claimed by Russia

Water Depth

0 m to 1,249 m

1,250 m to 2,499 m

2,500 m to 4,000 m

TAKEN FROM: Jeannette J. Lee, "New Seafloor Maps May Bolster U.S. Arctic Claims," *National Geographic News*, February 12, 2008, http://news.nationalgeographic.com/news/2008/02/080212-AP-arctic-grab.html (June 16, 2008).

advance its interests with other Arctic nations through venues such as the recent Arctic Ocean Conference in Ilulissat, Greenland.

Specifically, the United States should:

- *Create an interagency task force on the Arctic* bringing together the [U.S.] Departments of Defense, State, Interior, and Energy to develop the overall U.S. policy toward the region. The U.S. should use diplomatic, military, and economic means to maintain its sovereignty in the Arctic, including establishing a Joint Task Force-Arctic Region Command, headed by a Coast Guard flag officer. The U.S. should also establish an Arctic Coast Guard Forum modeled after the successful Northern Pacific Coast Guard Forum.

- *Accelerate the acquisition of icebreakers* to support the timely mapping of the Arctic OCS and the Arctic in general to advance U.S. national interests. The U.S. needs to swiftly map U.S. claims on the OCS and areas adjacent to Alaska to preserve its sovereign territorial rights. Timely mapping will be important as the other Arctic nations submit their claims within the 10-year window. The U.S. should not rely on mapping from other countries to advance its claims or to defend against the claims of other countries.

- *Provide the U.S. Coast Guard with a sufficient operations and maintenance budget* to support an increased, regular, and influential presence in the Arctic.

- *Reach out to Canada, Norway, Denmark, and—wherever possible—Russia.* Diplomacy and cooperation with Canada and European allies with interests in the region will be required to prevent conflict with Russia and to maintain the special relationship with Canada. The U.S.

needs to work with Canada to develop a mutually beneficial framework for the commercial exploitation of
Arctic hydrocarbons.

- *Create a public-private Arctic task force* to provide a formal avenue for the private sector to advise the U.S.
  government on Arctic economic development. This task
  force should include representatives from the energy,
  natural resources, and shipping sectors.

- *Authorize oil exploration and production* in the Arctic
  National Wildlife Refuge and other promising Arctic
  areas in order to expand domestic energy production.
  Congress should also streamline regulations for areas
  that it has already opened but heavily regulated.

As an Arctic nation, the United States has significant geopolitical and geo-economic interests in the High North. The
U.S. should not only have a place at the table, but also a leadership role in navigating the nascent [emerging] challenges
and opportunities, such as disputes over the Outer Continental Shelf, the navigation of Arctic sea-lanes, and commercial
development of natural resources and fisheries.

To play this role and to protect its interests, the U.S. needs
to revitalize its Arctic policy and commit the necessary resources to sustain America's leadership role in the High North.

> "Tom Hoefer [a mining company offi-
> cial stated], 'We are mining very suc-
> cessfully, very safely, protecting the en-
> vironment . . . and creating significant
> benefits for northern and Aboriginal
> peoples.'"

Polar Indigenous Peoples May Benefit from Resource Development

Felix von Geyer and Simon Handelsman

In the following viewpoint, the writers argue that indigenous peoples hold many of the mining rights in the Arctic and may use these rights to provide job opportunities and wealth for their communities. Further, including indigenous peoples in the process is a kind of "risk insurance" for the mining industry, according to the authors. Felix von Geyer is an environmental journalist from Montreal, and Simon Handelsman is a natural resources consultant based in New York.

Felix von Geyer and Simon Handelsman, "Poles Apart," *Mining Environment Management*, March 10, 2008, pp. 12–15. Copyright © 2009 Aspermont UK. All rights reserved. Reproduced by permission.

As you read, consider the following questions:

1. The agreement to develop diamond mines was preceded by what additional mining agreements with indigenous peoples, according to the authors?

2. According to von Geyer and Handelsman, where has a port been established that was made possible by ice-free summer seas?

3. What deepwater port is being refurbished for Canadian military Arctic patrol boats, according to the authors?

Regardless of climate change, the Arctic and Antarctic still form harsh environments for exploration and mining, and can be politically and environmentally sensitive. Human rights and other issues prevent the exploration and exploitation of uranium in Greenland, and it remains to be seen whether this political decision will change in the future. Similarly, the Sami indigenous people in Scandinavia's Arctic have prevented the exploitation of any minerals. Greenland's indigenous Inuit people may yet use mineral resources as a further reason to press for independence from Denmark.

Constitutional rights give Canada's aboriginal people recourse to consultation. Recent agreements to develop diamond mines were preceded by agreements for: uranium mines at Key Lake and Clough Lake in Saskatchewan; the Nanisivic lead-zinc mine on Baffin Island; and the Raglan polymetallic project in the extreme north Nunavik region of Quebec.

High aboriginal unemployment made the first Diavik diamond-mine agreement focus on job opportunities and later on developing locally owned business opportunities. This focus has since shifted to the community with a lump-sum payment being arranged to faciliate the purchase of equity in the development at favourable share prices. Such democratic participation is often seen to harbour increased costs to developers, but mine development in the Canadian Arctic demonstrates how elements of public participation can provide a form of risk insurance that is worth companies paying for.

While more than 150km south of the Arctic, [mining company] Rio Tinto's Diavik mine lies deep in the cold, treeless permafrost of Canada's Northwest Territories and reveals the benefits of undertaking responsible mineral exploration.

Benefits for Aboriginal Peoples

Tom Hoefer, Rio Tinto's manager for communications and external relations, [stated]: "We are mining very successfully, very safely, protecting the environment from significant adverse environmental effects, and creating significant benefits for northern and Aboriginal peoples."

Mr Hoefer stressed that Diavik surpassed C$1 billion [Canadian dollars] in Aboriginal business last year—one of only three mines in Canada to achieve this—and it enables Rio Tinto to meet further local commitments by hiring more Aboriginal workers. Now Canada's top diamond producer, Diavik achieved this through constructing "award-winning, engineered, rock 11 dykes to allow us to borrow the lake bottom to mine diamonds", he said. "Afterwards, we will return the mined areas back to lake, first building fish habitat within them. As a result, we will achieve Canada's fish policy of no net loss of fish habitat," he concluded.

Further development in the northern part of the Slave Geological Province in Canada's Arctic Circle would require major infrastructure. This might include a hydro-electric dam and reservoir complexes on several Arctic rivers, such as Coppermine, and high-voltage transmission lines and corridors would be required, as well as extending winter roads throughout the region, particularly up from Yellowknife, to serve mining facilities, particularly where global warming has put an end to traditional, year-round ice roads.

Ice-free summer seas, however, allow the establishment of a port on the Bathurst Inlet on the Arctic Circle, which would

Arctic Indigenous Peoples Benefit from Economic Development

Today, 169 Alaska Native Village corporations, formed under the federal Alaska Native Claims Settlement Act of 1971, operate from Prince William Sound to the Aleutians to the Arctic Slope, covering the state of Alaska, ranging from as small as 89 shareholders to more than 2,600. Besides investments in real estate and stock/bond portfolios, Native corporations now look to contracting and a variety of business options. With revenue and assets in the millions, these organizations have a huge impact on business in the state of Alaska.

*Barbara Morgan, "From Big to Small,
Alaska Native Village Corporations Are Thriving Today,"*
Alaska Business Monthly, *September 2005, pp. 52–56.*

see operational shipping in the summer months of July to October, passing around Baffin Island and into the Lancaster Sound.

Industry, Government and Inuits in Partnership

Such a project would require a public private partnership between the Inuit aboriginal peoples, industry and government, and funding upwards of C$237 million. The port and road would provide revenues from user fees and/or tolls, with road construction and operations possibly needing to be suspended between April and July to allow for migrating and breeding caribou herds.

Again, the rewards could be the uncovering of very high mineral potential, especially in base and precious metals, and even diamonds. Moreover, this port and road could help sustain Canada's northern diamond mines if it reduced the cost of shipping materials and fuel to them.

"Arctic deepwater ports are essential infrastructure that will do far more to support Canadian sovereignty claims than any military activity," says Stephen Priestley of Simon Fraser University's Canada-American Strategic Review. He also suggests that Western Arctic coal-gasification plans targeting the Tar Sands may also require exploitation of huge coal deposits on Ellesmere Island (not to mention lead and zinc at Nanisivik on Baffin Island).

Last summer [2007], Canada's Conservative Prime Minister, Stephen Harper, announced plans to refurbish the Arctic deepwater port at Nanisivik for his military Arctic patrol boats. Mr Priestley speculated that this could prove a logical spot to process that coal if gasification did happen. Harper's press secretary, Dimitri Soudas, said last year on Arctic sovereignty: "You either use it or lose it. We intend to use it."

Opportunities and Challenges

Yet, for all the jewels in the Arctic crown and possibly the Antarctic's own sceptred isle, as USGS [U.S. Geological Survey] research geologist Tim Collett stated, exploration will remain very difficult for the foreseeable future. Despite melting polar ice caps, the truth is that shipping and transport will remain ice-locked in the Arctic for some time to come, making it logistically diffcult to make a real dash for the Arctic.

However, the effect of climate change on the permafrost could result in adverse effects for mineral exploration. Mr Collett suggests that while the 30m or so relative topsoil of continuous permafrost in the stable Arctic has warmed only 1°C, the remaining permafrost can be anywhere from 600–900m deep.

However, according to Igor Holubec, geotechnical engineer and specialist advisor on arctic permafrost, the mean average air temperature has risen by 7°C over the past 100 years in the western Arctic and 17°C in the eastern Arctic.

He maintains that the mean average ground temperature has increased by an average of 16.9°C in the eastern Arctic and 6.3°C in the western Arctic. Environmentally, mine tailings and waste encapsulated in permafrost might be subject to movement or leakage, causing toxic waste to seep into groundwater.

Indeed, climate change offers an array of opportunities and challenges, but time alone will tell whether the Polar bull or bear will prevail.

"If this pipeline goes ahead then our people are not only going to suffer from not being able to hunt, fish and trap on our land; we will eventually lose control of our land."

Polar Indigenous Peoples Will Be Harmed by Resource Development

Macdonald Stainsby

In the following viewpoint, Macdonald Stainsby argues that a gas pipeline project in the Arctic will negatively impact the Dene and Inuvialuit peoples of Arctic Canada. The planned pipeline will bring natural gas from the Arctic to northern Alberta to support the tar sands industry, an industry that produces crude oil. Although some indigenous peoples have welcomed the jobs and money such a project would bring, most believe that it will destroy the caribou and fish populations they depend on for food, according to the author. Stainsby is a social justice activist who lives in Vancouver, British Columbia.

Macdonald Stainsby, "Indigenous Sovereignty and the MacKenzie Gas Project," *Briarpatch*, vol. 25, May 2006, pp. 19–21. Copyright © 2006 Briarpatch, Inc. Reproduced by permission.

As you read, consider the following questions:

1. What time limit has been placed on speakers at hearings concerning the Mackenzie gas project, and how does this differ from previous public debates about drilling in the region, according to Stainsby?

2. How much of the pipeline would cross the territory of the Deh Cho indigenous peoples?

3. For how long have the Dene been fighting to maintain their own sovereignty, according to the author?

The nations that control the largest oil reserves outside of Saudi Arabia—and I'm not talking about Iraq or Afghanistan—have seen their sovereignty violated and their most valuable resource taken from them for the benefit of corporations working hand-in-glove with an occupying power. I'm talking about the Dene and the Inuvialuit indigenous to northern Canada. These Arctic and sub-Arctic indigenous nations stand to be affected by the proposed MacKenzie Gas Project, a 1200 kilometre pipeline that, once in place, would feed the vast energy needs of the Alberta tar sands industry.

The tar sands already produce about forty percent of Canadian crude oil, but to keep up with growing demand, the industry will require a great deal of energy to separate the oil from the sand. The companies who have staked their claim in these sands are looking north for that energy, to the natural gas reserves of the Beaufort Sea and adjoining regions—the largest such untapped reserves of natural gas on the planet.

A Human, Environmental, and Cultural Disaster

The proposed Imperial Oil-led MacKenzie Gas Project seeks to use this natural gas, the cleanest-burning fossil fuel, to refine the bitumen into oil, the dirtiest fossil fuel. Economically, the plan is airtight: the gas will be sold after transport and make a profit for up to twenty years. In terms of human health, the environment, and the cultural survival of the affected nations, however, this plan is a disaster.

The proposed Mackenzie Gas Project would stretch from the Beaufort Delta to the northern border of Alberta, and would be the largest such industrial project in Canada's history. Before the tar-sands-derived crude is used to operate even a single lawn mower, however, the whole process will have already doubled Canada's greenhouse gas emissions, rendering moot all discussions of achieving our Kyoto treaty [an international environmental treaty] obligations.

Any developments in the Mackenzie Valley must follow a distinct environmental review process, as established though the the Gwich'in and Sahtu land claims in the Northwest Territories. The Mackenzie Valley Environmental Impact Review Board, consisting of half indigenous and half federal and territorial government representatives, assesses the environmental impacts of development projects and makes recommendations to the federal Minister. In August of 2004, the Minister of the Environment, in agreement with the Mackenzie Valley Environmental Impact Review Board and the Inuvialuit Game Council, appointed a Joint Review Panel for the MacKenzie Gas Project. The Joint Review Panel consists of four indigenous community members and three white professionals (a lawyer, a geographer and a geologist) who will evaluate the impacts of the project on the environment and lives of the people in the area.

In recent months, the joint Review Panel public hearings have begun traversing the communities of Dene and Inuvialuit up and down the Mackenzie Valley. These hearings are a hollow shell of the last such hearings, held from 1975–77 and chaired by then-Justice Thomas R. Berger in what was to be known as the Berger Inquiry. In that initial inquiry, Dene up and down the valley and elsewhere in the Northwest Territories were almost unanimous in their opposition to the project.

At that time, the panel traveled to each village, and stayed for as many days as were needed to hear the submissions of elders. Today, [2006] the hearings have earmarked less than a day for the most affected communities, and speakers are limited to fifteen minutes each.

Indigenous Concerns

Many of the concerns raised, however, remain unchanged. For many northerners, caribou and fish remain central to their ability to provide sustenance to their families and maintain their way of life. Some people fear the disruptions that development could herald: of a sudden massive inflow of money coinciding with the destruction of the traditional economy. While extensive resource-extraction bestows short-term gains at the cost of long-term sustainability, traditional practices have long maintained both the people and the land.

On August 5, 1975, in Fort Good Hope [in the Sahtu Region of the Northwest Territories], then-chief Frank T'Seleie said to the Berger Inquiry:

> We know that our grandchildren will speak a language that is their heritage, that has been passed on from before time. We know they will share their wealth and not hoard it, or keep it to themselves. We know they will look after their old people and respect them for their wisdom. We know they will look after this land and protect it and that five hundred years from now someone with skin my colour and moccasins on his feet will climb up the Ramparts and rest and look over the river and feel that he too has a place in the universe, and he will thank the same spirits that I thank, that his ancestors have looked after his land well, and he will be proud to be a Dene.
>
> It is for this unborn child, Mr. Berger, that my nation will stop the pipeline. It is so that this unborn child can know the freedom of this land that I am willing to lay down my life.

Oil Drilling Will Threaten Indigenous Peoples

The Inupiat, relatives of the Inuit who inhabit other parts of the Arctic, fear oil spills or drilling activity will disrupt the endangered bowhead whales and other marine animals that they have hunted for generations.

"We want to continue to survive. Our lives are tied to subsistence. So is our culture and our religion with all the animals," said Jack Schaefer, president of the Inupiat village of Point Hope.

Robert Campbell,
"Arctic Oil Bonanza Worries Alaska Natives,"
Reuters, *February 26, 2008. www.commondreams.org.*

Indigenous Peoples Formerly Supported the Project

Until very recently, the image southerners have been fed is a united indigenous population supportive of the proposed Mackenzie Gas Project and at loggerheads with environmentalists. The Northwest Territorial government trumpets that the pipeline could open the whole western Arctic to industrial development, and the project could provide up to 20,000 person-years of employment in the region, as well as lucrative returns from increasingly scarce gas resources. As indigenous communities have long been impoverished by development that has long excluded their interests and degraded their traditional livelihoods, now many indigenous leaders clamour for the opportunity to share in the bounty being stripped from their lands. This is exemplified by the existence of the Aboriginal Pipeline Group, a subsidized portion of the project involving some of the leaderships of the Inuvialuit (Inuit),

Gwich'in (Dene) and Sahtu (Dene) nations (Frank T'Seleie himself is now one of the Aboriginal Pipeline Group's leading proponents).

However, since the beginning of the contemporary hearings, there are indications that some community members are questioning rather than deferring to the judgment of their leaders. In an open letter to *The Yellowknifer*, Roberta A. Alexie wrote on February 6, 2006:

> When I think about the pipeline, all I see for my future are problems. And I see leaders standing by and not helping our people. Money seems to be the only issue here. What about the conditions of our communities? The money will not last forever, but our people will be here for generations. We have a beautiful land and the power to protect it. Why are we going to put a pipeline through it? Why are we going to destroy whatever habitat we have for the sake of a pipeline? I don't think any of this is worth the money that the governments or the industrial corporations will give.

Opposition to the Project

For years, the wildcard in the Crown's efforts to secure access for the pipeline has been the lack of a final settlement between the Crown and the Deh Cho (Dene) nation. Forty percent of the pipeline would traverse the territory of the Deh Cho, who have been the strongest opponents of the proposed pipeline. A previous Deh Cho lawsuit claiming the pipeline environmental review failed to adequately account for Deh Cho interests was settled last summer for $31.5 million, but a new lawsuit was launched last month challenging a January decision by the Mackenzie Valley Environmental Impact Review Board.

A year ago [2005], the proposed MacKenzie Gas Project had been required to negotiate access and benefit agreements with the Deh Cho communities directly. But the January ruling of the Review Board reversed this requirement following discussions between the Department of Indian Affairs and Northern Development and Imperial Oil. Many Deh Cho perceive their exclusion from these meetings as a violation of the government's duty to consult with indigenous nations (even with nations where there is no "final settlement") before moving ahead with development.

The Gas Project Will Be the First of Many

The Mackenzie valley is one of the few primarily untouched pristine areas left on Turtle Island. Should it go through, the MacKenzie Gas Project would be not the end of development for the valley, but the beginning. As old natural gas fields run dry, new fields will need to be set up. Pipelines and new highways will open up other development schemes, from hydro projects to mining.

For thirty years the Dene have been resisting attempts to subvert their sovereignty, and now, at the eleventh hour of the proposed pipeline, many have begun to question the entire process of industrializing the North for the benefit of southern oil companies. For them, the social and environmental costs are simply too high. As Tom Laviolette of Hay River, Northwest Territories, wrote on April 3, 2006:

"If this pipeline goes ahead then our people are not only going to suffer from not being able to hunt, fish and trap on our land; we will eventually lose control of our land. It will be destroyed by oil and mining companies.

"Just think of how it is when you take a drive down south to the cities. Everywhere you look it's fenced off and some white farmer owns the land. If that's what you want, then go for it. [. . . .]

"I can't believe this is happening. Where are our supposed native leaders in all of this? They must be far too close to the owners of the oil and gas companies to realize what their own people want."

The cost of tar sands extraction is usually only measured in the massive destruction of ecosystems in northern Alberta. Yet there is no way this project can move forward without devastating land from the Arctic Ocean south to the Alberta border, further impoverishing the northern indigenous nations of Denendeh/the Northwest Territories, and taking the resources of Dene and Inuvialuit along with the land and resources of the various indigenous nations of northern Alberta.

"It's time to drill again here in America—while conserving more and pursuing new energy technologies for the future."

The United States Must Drill for Oil in the Arctic

Paul Driessen

In the following viewpoint, Paul Driessen argues that drilling for oil in the Arctic is vital to the economy of the United States because it will serve to stabilize energy markets worldwide. He further contends that current technology can preserve the environment while extracting oil. He also argues that drilling in the Arctic National Wildlife Refuge (ANWR) will add billions of dollars and many jobs to the U.S. economy, concluding that environmental activists do not have the right to deny the country such energy gains. Driessen is a senior fellow with the Committee For A Constructive Tomorrow and the Center for the Defense of Free Enterprise, both in Washington, D.C.

As you read, consider the following questions:

1. According to the viewpoint, what state is comparable in size to the Arctic National Wildlife Refuge?

2. What other natural resources does the United States have "locked up," according to Driessen?

3. How much oil does the Geological Survey and Congressional Research Service predict is located beneath ANWR, according to Driessen?

"We can't drill our way out of our energy problem." This daily mantra, mostly from Democrats, underscores an abysmal grasp of economics by the politicians, activists, bureaucrats and judges who are dictating US policies. If only their hot air could be converted into usable energy.

Drilling is no silver bullet. But it is vital. It won't generate overnight production. But just announcing that America is finally hunting oil again would send a powerful signal to energy markets—and to speculators—many of whom are betting that continued US drilling restrictions will further exacerbate the global demand-supply imbalance, and send "futures" prices even higher.

Pro-drilling policies would likely bring lower prices, as did recent announcements that Brazil had found new offshore oil fields and Iraq would sign contracts to increase oil production. Conversely, news that supplies are tightening—because of sabotage in Nigeria's delta region, or more congressional bans on leasing—will send prices upward.

Alaska Has Oil

One of our best prospects is Alaska's Arctic National Wildlife Refuge [ANWR] which geologists say contains billions of barrels of recoverable oil. If President [Bill] Clinton hadn't bowed to Wilderness Society demands and vetoed 1995 legislation, we'd be producing a million barrels a day from ANWR right now. That's equal to US imports from Saudi Arabia, at $50 billion annually.

Drilling in ANWR would get new oil flowing in 5–10 years, depending on how many lawsuits environmentalists file. That's

Wildlife Can Be Protected

Oil production would inevitably affect the refuge [ANWR]. But studies at Prudhoe Bay to the west, where oil has been produced since 1977 in an area more than twice the size of the one planned for ANWR, show that the effects can be minimized and wildlife protected, particularly with today's newer exploration technology.

"Our View on Energy Policy,"
USA Today, *June 10, 2008. www.usatoday.com.*

far faster than benefits would flow from supposed alternatives: devoting millions more acres of cropland to corn or cellulosic ethanol, converting our vehicle fleet to hybrid and flex-fuel cars, building dozens of new nuclear power plants, and blanketing thousands of square miles with wind turbines and solar panels. These alternatives would take decades to implement, and all face political, legal, technological, economic and environmental hurdles.

ANWR is the size of South Carolina. Its narrow coastal plain is frozen and windswept most of the year. Wildlife flourish amid drilling and production in other Arctic regions, and would do so near ANWR facilities. Inuits who live there know this, and support drilling by an 8:1 margin. Gwich'in Indians who oppose drilling live hundreds of miles away—and have leased and drilled their own tribal lands, including caribou migratory routes.

Drilling and production operations would impact only 2,000 acres—to produce 15 billion gallons of oil annually. Saying this tiny footprint would spoil the refuge is like saying a major airport along South Carolina's northern border would destroy the state's scenery and wildlife.

Better to Drill

It's a far better bargain than producing 7 billion gallons of ethanol in 2007 from corn grown on an area the size of Indiana (23 million acres). It's far better than using wind to generate enough electricity to power New York City, which would require blanketing Connecticut (3 million acres) with turbines.

Anti-drilling factions also assert: "US energy prices are high, because Americans consume 25% of the world's oil, while possessing only 3% of its proven oil reserves."

Possession has nothing to do with prices—any more than owning a library, but never opening the books, improves intellectual abilities; or owning farmland that's never tilled feeds hungry people.

It is production that matters—and the United States has locked up vast energy resources. Not just an estimated 169 billion barrels of oil in the Outer Continental Shelf, Rockies, Great Lakes, Southwest and ANWR—but also natural gas, coal, uranium and hydroelectric resources.

"Proven reserves" are resources that drilling has confirmed exist and can be produced with current technology and prices. By imposing bans on leasing, and encouraging environmentalists to challenge seismic and drilling permits on existing leases, politicians ensure that we will never increase our proven reserves. In fact, reserves will decrease, as we deplete existing deposits and don't replace them. The rhetoric is clever—but disingenuous, fraudulent and harmful.

The Geological Survey and Congressional Research Service say it's 95% likely that there are 15.6 billion barrels of oil beneath ANWR. With today's prices and technology, 60% of that is recoverable. At $135 a barrel, that represents $1.3 trillion that we would not have to send to Iran, Russia, Saudi Arabia and Venezuela. It means lower prices and reduced risks of oil spills from tankers carrying foreign crude.

The Benefits of Drilling

It represents another $400 billion in state and federal royalties and corporate income taxes—plus billions in lease sale revenues, plus thousands of direct and indirect jobs, in addition to numerous jobs created when this $1.7 trillion total is invested in the USA.

It means additional billions in income tax revenues that those jobs would generate, and new opportunities for minority, poor and blue collar families to improve their lives and living standards. It means lower prices for gasoline, heating, cooling, food and other products.

That's just ANWR. Factor in America's other locked-up energy, and we're talking tens of trillions of dollars that we either keep in the United States, by producing that energy . . . or ship overseas.

This energy belongs to all Americans. It's not the private property of environmental pressure groups, or of politicians who cater to them in exchange for re-election support.

This energy is likewise the common heritage of mankind. Politicians and eco-activists have no right to keep it off limits—and tell the rest of the world: We have no intention of developing American energy. We don't care if you need oil, soaring food and energy prices are pummeling your poor, or drilling in your countries harms your habitats to produce oil for US consumers.

Those attitudes are immoral and intolerable. It's time to drill again here in America—while conserving more and pursuing new energy technologies for the future.

> *"Opening the Arctic Refuge to energy development is about transferring our public estate into corporate hands so that it can be liquidated for a quick buck."*

The United States Should Not Drill for Oil in the Arctic

Natural Resources Defense Council

In the following viewpoint, the Natural Resources Defense Council (NRDC) argues that the Arctic National Wildlife Refuge (ANWR) should not be drilled for oil. The writers contend that Arctic drilling will not lower gasoline prices and will damage irreversibly ANWR because the oil fields are scattered throughout the refuge. The NDRC asserts that if ANWR is drilled, it will soon look like the oil complex at Prudhoe Bay, Alaska, with its many contaminated waste sites. The NRDC is a nonprofit organization concerned with preserving wildlife and the environment. The following viewpoint has been edited from its original version.

"Arctic National Wildlife Refuge: Why Trash an American Treasure for a Tiny Percentage of Our Oil Needs?" Natural Resources Defense Council, July 16, 2008. Reproduced with permission from the Natural Resources Defense Council.

As you read, consider the following questions:

1. According to a poll taken in June 2008, what percentage of Americans supported protecting the Arctic Refuge?

2. How much per gallon of gas would be saved at the gas pumps over the course of twenty years if ANWR were drilled for oil, according to the Energy Information Agency?

3. What is the solution to America's energy problems, according to the NRDC?

On the northern edge of our continent, stretching from the peaks of the Brooks Range across a vast expanse of tundra to the Beaufort Sea, lies Alaska's Arctic National Wildlife Refuge [ANWR]. An American Serengeti [a large wildlife area in Africa], the Arctic Refuge continues to pulse with million-year-old ecological rhythms. It is the greatest living reminder that conserving nature in its wild state is a core American value.

A Clear Desire to Protect the Arctic

In affirmation of that value, Congress and the American people have consistently made clear their desire to protect this treasure and rejected claims that drilling for oil in the Arctic Refuge is any sort of answer to the nation's dependence on foreign oil. Twice in 2005, Congress acted explicitly to defend the refuge from the [George W.] Bush administration and pro-drilling forces, with House leaders removing provisions that would have allowed for drilling from a massive budget bill, and the Senate withstanding an attempt by Republican leaders to open up the Arctic.

Since then, concerned Americans have continued to push Congress to thwart recurring efforts to see the refuge spoiled. But in the face of soaring gas prices, President Bush has once again offered up Arctic drilling as a solution for America's energy crisis, despite evidence from the government itself that drilling wouldn't make a dent in the price we pay at the pump. Instead, the president is again ignoring the science and valuing oil and gas interests over America's precious natural heritage. In this continuing battle, America's premier wildlife sanctuary is at stake.

Americans Have Steadily Opposed Drilling the Arctic National Wildlife Refuge

The controversy over drilling in the Arctic Refuge—the last piece of America's Arctic coastline not already open to oil exploration—isn't new. Big Oil has long sought access to the refuge's coastal plain, a fragile swath of tundra that teems with staggering numbers of birds and animals. During the Bush administration's first term, repeated attempts were made to open the refuge. But time after time, the American public rejected the idea.

Congress has received hundreds of thousands of emails, faxes and phone calls from citizens opposed to drilling in the Arctic Refuge, an outpouring that has helped make the difference. And polls have consistently shown that a majority of Americans oppose drilling, even in the face of high gas prices and misleading claims from oil interests. A June 2008 poll by the research firm Belden Russonello & Stewart found that 55 percent of the American public supports continued protection for the Arctic Refuge, and only 35 percent of Americans believe that allowing oil companies to drill in the refuge would result in lower gas prices for American consumers.

Despite repeated failure and stiff opposition, drilling proponents press on. Why? They believe that opening the Arctic Refuge will turn the corner in the broader national debate over whether or not energy, timber, mining and other industries should be allowed into pristine wild areas across the country. Along with the Arctic, oil interests are now tar-

Drilling in the Arctic Will Not Solve the Oil Crisis

The U.S. Energy Information Administration (EIA) has concluded that at its peak in 2030, oil from the Arctic refuge would only lower gas prices by a few pennies per gallon. The EIA also estimated that peak production in 2025 with new access along our coasts would produce a meager 220,000 barrels per day and only for a limited time. By contrast increasing fuel efficiency to 35 mpg by 2020 we would decrease demand by 1 million barrels of oil per day indefinitely.

"Addressing High Gas Prices,"
Defenders of Wildlife, Aug. 8, 2008. www.defenders.org.

geting America's protected coastal waters. Next up: Greater Yellowstone? Our Western canyonlands?

The drive to drill in the Arctic Refuge is about oil company profits and lifting barriers to future exploration in protected lands, pure and simple. It has nothing to do with energy independence. Opening the Arctic Refuge to energy development is about transferring our public estate into corporate hands so that it can be liquidated for a quick buck.

Arctic Refuge Oil Is a Distraction, Not a Solution

What would America gain by allowing heavy industry into the refuge? Very little. Oil from the refuge would hardly make a dent in our dependence on foreign imports—leaving our economy and way of life just as exposed to wild swings in worldwide oil prices and supply as it is today. The truth is, we simply can't drill our way to energy independence.

Although drilling proponents often say there are 16 billion barrels of oil under the refuge's coastal plain, the U.S. Geological Service's estimate of the amount that could be recovered economically—that is, the amount likely to be profitably extracted and sold—represents less than a year's U.S. supply.

It would take 10 years for any Arctic Refuge oil to reach the market, and even when production peaks—in the distant year of 2027—the refuge would produce a paltry 3 percent of Americans' daily consumption. The U.S. government's own Energy Information Agency recently reported that drilling in the Arctic would save less than 4 cents per gallon in 20 years. Whatever oil the refuge might produce is simply irrelevant to the larger issue of meeting America's future energy needs.

Handing On to Future Generations a Wild, Pristine Arctic? Priceless.

Oil produced from the Arctic Refuge would come at an enormous, and irreversible, cost. The refuge is among the world's last true wildernesses, and it is one of the largest sanctuaries for Arctic animals. Traversed by a dozen rivers and framed by jagged peaks, this spectacular wilderness is a vital birthing ground for polar bears, grizzlies, Arctic wolves, caribou and the endangered shaggy musk ox, a mammoth-like survivor of the last Ice Age.

For a sense of what Big Oil's heavy machinery would do to the refuge, just look 60 miles west to Prudhoe Bay—a gargantuan oil complex that has turned 1,000 square miles of fragile tundra into a sprawling industrial zone containing 1,500 miles of roads and pipelines, 1,400 producing wells and three jetports. The result is a landscape defaced by mountains of sewage sludge, scrap metal, garbage and more than 60 contaminated waste sites that contain—and often leak—acids, lead, pesticides, solvents and diesel fuel.

While proponents of drilling insist that the Arctic Refuge could be developed by disturbing as little as 2,000 acres within the 1.5-million-acre coastal plain, an NRDC [National Resources Defense Council] analysis reveals this to be pure myth. Why? Because U.S. Geological Survey studies have found that oil in the refuge isn't concentrated in a single, large reservoir. Rather, it's spread across the coastal plain in more than 30 small deposits, which would require vast networks of roads and pipelines that would fragment the habitat, disturbing and displacing wildlife.

A Responsible Path to Energy Security

The solution to America's energy problems will be found in American ingenuity, not more oil. Only by reducing our reliance on oil—foreign and domestic—and investing in cleaner, renewable forms of power will our country achieve true energy security.

The good news is that we already have many of the tools we need to accomplish this. For example, Detroit has the technology right now to produce high-performance hybrid cars, trucks and SUVs. If America made the transition to these more efficient vehicles, far more oil would be saved than the Arctic Refuge is likely to produce. Doesn't that make far more sense than selling out our natural heritage and exploiting one of our true wilderness gems?

Periodical Bibliography

The following articles have been selected to supplement the diverse views presented in this chapter.

Australian Antarctic Division	"Experience Antarctica: Fact Files," July 25, 2008. www.aad.gov.au.
James Barnes	"Why the White Wilderness Needs Our Care," *BBC News*, March 31, 2008. news.bbc.uk.
Anthony Bergin and Marcus Haward	"Frozen Assets: Securing Australia's Antarctic Future," *Strategic Insights*, vol. 34, April 2007.
Bernard P. Herber	"Protecting the Antarctic Commons," Udall Center for Studies in Public Policy, 2007.
Indian and Northern Affairs Canada	"Economic Development in British Columbia: Fact Sheet," October 30, 2008. www.ainc-inac.ca.
D.K. Leary	"Bi-Polar Disorder? Is Bioprospecting an Issue for the Arctic as Well as Antarctica?" *Review of European Community and International Environmental Law*, 2008.
Michael Macrander and Ian M. Voparil	"Shell Moves to Protect Marine Mammals Offshore Alaska," *Offshores*, vol. 68, no. 9, September 2008.
Lisa Murkowski	Arctic Forum Speech, Center for Strategic and International Studies, July 23, 2008. www.csis.org.
Ed Struzkik	"The Arctic Resource Rush Is On," *Environment 360*, July 10, 2008.
Shingo Takazawa	"Alaska Native, Eskimo Whaling," Japan Whaling Association, *ISANA*, no. 32, December 2005.

CHAPTER 4

What Role Should Tourism Play in the North and South Poles?

Chapter Preface

A growing trend in the tourist industry is deeply impacting the regions surrounding both the North and South Poles. The concept of "extreme tourism" is driven by some people's desire to go to remote and inaccessible places to hike, climb, kayak, or to engage in other sports. Patrick Barkham, writing in the July 9, 2008, issue of *The Guardian*, calls these people "trophy tourists," those who want "to tick off ever more extreme locations on their global adventures."

Because both the Arctic and the Antarctic are challenging places to visit, an increasing number of extreme tourists are booking trips to these locations. In the Arctic, tourists are finding their way to remote indigenous villages to learn first-hand about survival in the north. They are signing up to kayak among icebergs and watch whales up close. In 2008, a record number of cruise ships traveled to the Canadian Arctic. In the Antarctic, an even more forbidding environment, tourists are booking passages on cruise ships traveling to the southernmost continent. Most of these cruises also promise an actual landing on the shore so that the tourist can observe up close the flora and fauna of the region.

Tourism in the polar regions, however, is fraught with controversy. As Barkham notes, "Bundled in with our desire to impress with obscure locations and find our authentic selves in the mirror of foreign societies are concerns about travel, the environment, and climate change. It all collides in Antarctica." Indeed, now that some 50,000 tourists a year are making their way to the Antarctic, it is nearly impossible for them not to impact the fragile environment of the polar region. Many scientists worry about the long-term damage tourists will do to this formerly pristine environment. Extreme tourism, while an exciting adventure for the tourist, can destroy the very location the extreme tourist wishes to visit.

In addition, traveling to such a remote and inaccessible location is not always safe. For example, in January 2005, extreme tourist Stephen Thomas fell into a crevasse while climbing on what appeared to be safe looking slopes on Wiencke Island. Although he was an experienced climber and sailor, and although his fellow climbers were able to extricate him and return him to a cruise ship, Thomas later died from his injuries. According to the January 2006 issue of *International Travel News*, Thomas underestimated the dangers of hiking in Antarctica, and made several errors that cost him his life.

Other tourists similarly experienced how dangerous and unpredictable travel in Antarctica can be. In November 2007, the *Explorer*, a long-time, ice-strengthened cruise ship, sank off the coast of Antarctica. Because there were other ships in the vicinity and the weather was calm, all passengers were rescued. Nonetheless, many more cruise vessels are plying Antarctic waters now, and most of them are not as well prepared as the *Explorer* and their crew, according to E.J. Steward and D. Draper, writing in the June 2008 issue of *Arctic*.

On the other hand, Geoffrey Baldacchino in his 2006 book, *Extreme Tourism: Lessons from the World's Cold Water Islands*, argues that "there is sufficient environmental awareness, legislation and training for protecting natural assets" in the cold water islands he studied, including locations in the far north and the far south. Indeed, there is considerable evidence that people who have visited Antarctica and the Arctic return home with renewed zeal for protecting the polar environment. Moreover, tourist organizations such as the International Association of Antarctic Tour Operators work hard to supervise and certify safe, sustainable tourism in these fragile regions. It is unclear whether such efforts are sufficient to keep people and the environment safe, including those tourists seeking extreme experiences.

> *"Tourism must be subject to some constraints, and it must not compromise Antarctica's established designation as a natural reserve, devoted to peace and science."*

Tourism Must Be Better Regulated in Antarctica

The Antarctic and Southern Ocean Coalition

In the following viewpoint, writers from the Antarctic and Southern Ocean Coalition (ASOC) report that tourism in Antarctica is increasing rapidly. They express concern that tourism is not regulated in Antarctica and argue that the Antarctic Treaty System must take responsibility for regulating the tourist trade in Antarctica to preserve the environment. Although tour operators have been well-intentioned thus far, ASOC argues, they are motivated by profit and self-interest, and thus must come under scrutiny and reasonable regulation. ASOC is a global coalition of more than one hundred environmental organizations devoted to preserving and protecting Antarctica and its waters.

As you read, consider the following questions:

1. How many tourists visited Antarctica in the 1990–1991 season, according to the viewpoint?

2. What key Antarctic states have recognized the importance of tourism regulation, according to ASOC?

3. Who has funded the ASOC Antarctic Tourism Campaign since 2002?

If you are planning a trip to Antarctica, read about ASOC's [Antarctic and Southern Ocean Coalition's] Antarctica Tourism Campaign, which supports regulation of commercial Antarctic tourism. ASOC is concerned about the rapid growth of commercial tourism, which presently is not regulated by the Environment Protocol, including size of ships, number of visitors to various areas, on-shore infrastructure development, use of helicopters and other issues that affect the environment. Note that ASOC is not opposed to tourism but does believe that it should not be left unregulated.

ASOC's Antarctic Tourist Campaign

Although Antarctic tourism began in the late 1950s, it remained at low levels until the early 1990s when it took off. From a base of 4,698 tourists in the 1990/91 summer, annual numbers have risen to 24,281 in the summer of 2003/04. But if one adds the staff and crew to the passengers, the figure for 2003/04 has been calculated as 44,266. Although tourist residence time is shorter, this means that vastly more tourists than scientists and support staff on national programs now visit the Antarctic each year. Industry figures project a continuing increase in tourism numbers through this decade.

Although the majority of these tourists still travel in small-medium sized vessels, the industry is rapidly diversifying. Large passenger vessels (without any ice-strengthening) capable of carrying up to 800 passengers (and with correspondingly large crews) are now active in the Antarctic. Mass-tourism has arrived. Alongside this, niche-marketed "adventure tourism" has developed—just about anything you may want to do involving aqualungs, parachutes, skis, motorbikes, etc. can now be pandered to by commercial operators. Large numbers of people now land at key wildlife and historic sites in Antarctica and, increasingly, light aircraft, helicopters and all-terrain vehicles allow penetration further in from the coast. So-called "fly-sail" operations, whereby tourists are ferried by aircraft to ships in Antarctica, thus increasing the throughput of passengers, have commenced in the past two seasons.

Within a relatively short time, as the numbers of tourists continue to increase, and as the present Soviet-era fleet chartered by the tourism industry reaches obsolescence, we may see the emergence of air-supported mass tourism in Antarctica—and the concomitant calls for accommodation ashore, airstrips, etc. The problems of tourism, familiar everywhere else, have arrived in Antarctica, and ASOC is making the point that this requires the sorts of checks and controls that the tourism industry reasonably has to accept just about everywhere else. The alternative is a free-for-all.

Tourism Must Be Regulated

What makes Antarctica a particular concern is that there is no regulation of tourism at present. Apart from an obligation to conduct prior Environmental Impact Assessment—which tourism operators, like everybody else are expected to do—there is essentially no constraint on where you can go, what you can do, and how many of you can do it.

The practical consequence of this is that tourism is already exerting pressures on the Antarctic environment, and the increasing commercial interest is changing the nature of the Antarctic political regime. Increasingly, commercial benefit, rather than concern for the environment, science, or international cooperation, is driving the Antarctic political regime.

"Polar expeditions are easy now! Thanks to global warming." Cartoon by Bill Proud. www.CartoonStock.com.

This (coupled with similar trends in fishing, lingering interest in minerals and an emerging interest in bioprospecting) threatens to unpick the delicate accommodation on sovereignty at the heart of the 1959 Antarctic Treaty.

Remarkably, for close to a decade after the adoption of the Protocol no state sought to seriously examine the Antarctic tourism industry or suggest any need to effectively regulate it. In the absence of such interest, the industry developed an entrenched and influential position in the Antarctic Treaty system. Encouragingly, a number of key Antarctic states (led by France and New Zealand) have recently recognised the importance of tourism regulation. But the industry, and its association (IAATO [International Association of Antarctic Tour Operators]) still argue that industry "self-regulation" is all that is required.

ASOC has argued that this is certainly not adequate, nor equitable. Over the past several years ASOC has argued that the Antarctic Treaty states must take responsibility for regulating Antarctic tourism, in order to secure the Antarctic environment and protect the political stability of the Antarctic Treaty system. Whatever the good intentions of present industry members, the nature of commercial tourism is such that its unrepresentative nature, self-interest and structural instability make it an inappropriate sole guardian for some 10% of the surface of the earth.

With generous funding from the Goldman Foundation since 2002, ASOC has been able to establish a dedicated Antarctic Tourism Campaign focused on raising public awareness of the issues posed by Antarctic tourism, and putting the case for appropriate regulation of the industry before Antarctic states and the Antarctic Treaty system.

Our case is not that there should be a prohibition of Antarctic tourism. It is a legitimate activity. But its legitimacy is contingent. Tourism must be subject to some constraints, and it must not compromise Antarctica's established designation as a natural reserve, devoted to peace and science. If it is not to become a destructive facet of human activity in Antarctica, it cannot increase endlessly and it has to accept some limits on the types and locations of activities.

"The trend of increasing visitor numbers has led the Antarctic Treaty countries to establish guidelines and regulations to minimise the impact of . . . visitors on this remarkable environment."

Tourism Is Well-Regulated in Antarctica

Rebecca Roper-Gee

In the following viewpoint, Rebecca Roper-Gee discusses the growth in the number of tourists traveling to Antarctica, asserting that the Antarctic Treaty countries have established guidelines and regulations to ensure that visitors do not harm the environment. She contends that the Environmental Protocol requires that tour operators must complete environmental impact assessments before bringing visitors to the continent. In addition, she argues, the International Association of Antarctic Tour Operators (IAATO) has guidelines that ensure safety and environmental protection. Roper-Gee writes for the Antarctica New Zealand Web site.

As you read, consider the following questions:

1. According to the author, what happened in a 1979 over-flight of Antarctica?

2. What do Chile and New Zealand require of ships going to Antarctica, according to Roper-Gee?

3. How many members does IAATO have, and how does the organization affect the tourism industry?

There is no doubt Antarctica is an incredible tourist destination. It is a magnificent and largely uninhabited wilderness with majestic mountains, glaciers, icebergs and abundant wildlife. Its remoteness, inaccessibility and severe climate add an element of adventure to a visit to Antarctica. Visitor numbers have increased rapidly over the last few decades. In 2002/2003, 13,571 tourists visited Antarctica, compared with only 6,000 ten years ago. Only 5% of these tourists have visited the Ross Sea region of Antarctica, where New Zealand's national programme activity is focussed. The majority of tours are to the Antarctic Peninsula region, close to South America.

Tours are organised by private companies and people from all over the world make the journey to see the icy continent. The majority of tourists come from the USA, followed by Germany, Britain and Australia.

The trend of increasing visitor numbers has led the Antarctic Treaty countries to establish guidelines and regulations to minimise the impact of these visitors on this remarkable environment.

Flights to Antarctica

Tourists began to visit Antarctica by air in the 1950s when flights over the Antarctic Peninsula were made. In the 1960s commercial flights landed at McMurdo Sound and the South Pole.

Regular overflights ran between 1977 and 1980, with over 11,000 people taking the trip from Australia and New Zealand.

At a meeting in 1979 Antarctic Treaty Nations expressed concern at the danger of flying in the turbulent Antarctic atmosphere where there was a lack of radio beacons, meteorological stations and emergency services. Later that year, 257 people were killed when one of these overflights struck Mt Erebus in poor visibility. Overflights were resumed in 1994 by an Australian airline.

Other companies have also begun to make flights over the continent and to the northern tip of the Antarctic Peninsula from South America. There are also businesses, which arrange flights for private climbing expeditions and trips to the South Pole. In 2002/2003, over 1,500 tourists flew over Antarctica without landing, and 300 made aircraft landings.

Ship-Borne Tourists

Ship visits by tourists also began in the 1950s with an Argentinean vessel, which took 100 passengers to the Antarctic Peninsula. In 1968 a chartered ship visited the Ross Sea with 24 people.

Since then, cruise ships have regularly visited the Antarctic Peninsula, operating from Argentina and Chile. It is one of the most popular areas to visit because of its proximity to South America, its warmer climate, abundant wildlife and many research stations, which are visited by some tours.

Several cruise ships now also operate in the Ross Sea area, operating from Bluff, Lyttelton or Hobart as well as from South America. In recent seasons, about 500 people have taken these trips, which last from two to four weeks. Landings are made in zodiacs (small inflatable rubber boats) at locations such as Cape Adare, Possession Island, Scott Base, McMurdo and Terra Nova Bay Stations, Cape Evans and Cape Royds. Helicopter trips are regularly made from one of the ships for overflights and to visit locations such as Taylor Valley in the McMurdo Dry Valleys.

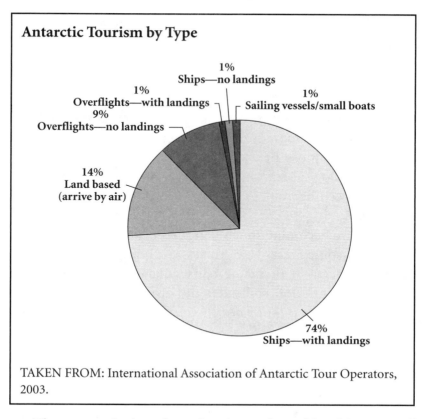

Antarctic Tourism by Type

1%
Ships—no landings

1%
Overflights—with landings

1%
Sailing vessels/small boats

9%
Overflights—no landings

14%
Land based
(arrive by air)

74%
Ships—with landings

TAKEN FROM: International Association of Antarctic Tour Operators, 2003.

The vast majority of tourism is conducted by ship. A small number of yachts also visit Antarctica each year, some with fee-paying passengers. There are currently no permanent land-based facilities constructed for tourism.

Impact of Tourism

Although remoteness and lack of development make Antarctica a difficult and expensive place to visit, there is no shortage of people wanting to make the trip—tourist numbers now exceed the number of scientists and support staff who work there, and are increasing steadily. However, the length of time spent ashore is much less than by programme personnel. Although visits are usually short, they are concentrated into a small number of landing sites, creating potential for cumulative impacts in the long term.

Some consider tourists an environmental pressure Antarctica could do without. Others note that the tourists are generally well informed and concerned about the Antarctic environment and usually become very good advocates for the protection of Antarctica when they return home.

Poorly managed visitors of any kind (whether paying tourists or national programme personnel) can cause damage to slow growing moss beds, disturb wildlife and take historic items or geological souvenirs. Rubbish and wastes from ships have also been a problem, as have unplanned visits to scientific bases.

Visits are becoming much better regulated, and impact has reduced in some areas. Nevertheless, with any operation, accidents can occur with major consequences for the environment, such as the oil spill after the grounding of the tourist and supply ship *Bahia Paraiso* on the Antarctic Peninsula [1989].

Regulations on Tourism

The Environmental Protocol to the Antarctic Treaty applies the same requirements to any type of activity, including tourism. Under the Protocol, organisers of Antarctic activities are required to complete an environmental impact assessment (EIA). The EIA describes the activities of the operator and helps to identify and reduce possible impacts of the tourists on the environment. Environmental monitoring is being used at some sites in the Antarctic Peninsula area to detect environmental changes caused by visitors.

In 1994 the Treaty countries made further recommendations on tourism and non-government activities. This "Guidance for Visitors to the Antarctic" is intended to help visitors become aware of their responsibilities under the Treaty and Protocol. The document concerns the protection of Antarctic wildlife and protected areas, the respecting of scientific research, personal safety and impact on the environment. Guidelines have also been written for the organisers of tourist and private ventures—these require prior notification of the trip to the organiser's national authority (e.g. Antarctica New Zealand), assessment of potential environmental impacts, the ability to cope with environmental emergencies such as oil spills, self-sufficiency, the proper disposal of wastes and respect for the Antarctic environment and research activities. The guidelines outline detailed procedures to be followed during the planning of the trip, when in the Antarctic Treaty area and on completion of the trip.

Individual countries have also introduced measures to minimise effects of tourists. Chile requires all captains of ships that go to Antarctica to attend a month-long school in Antarctic navigation. New Zealand sends a government representative on all ships visiting the Ross Dependency to supervise visits to the historic huts and Scott Base and to observe how well the provisions of the treaty and protocol are adhered to.

The Role of the International Association of Antarctic Tour Operators (IAATO)

Tourist operators in Antarctica have organised an association (the International Association of Antarctic Tour Operators) to promote safety and environmental responsibility amongst cruise operators. Their objectives include working within the Antarctic Treaty System and other international agreements such as MARPOL and SOLAS and fostering cooperation between private-sector travel and the international scientific community in the Antarctic. A very significant IAATO policy is that itineraries should be planned in such a way that no more than 100 people are ashore at a time at any one site.

IAATO drafted the documents which formed the basis of "Guidance for Visitors to the Antarctic", Antarctic Treaty Recommendation XVIII-I. Since 1991 when IAATO was established, its membership has grown from seven operators to more than 40. The members meet annually and have added

"*[The Antarctic Treaty System] needs to set a sensible limit to the number of visitors [to Antarctica] in a year.*"

The Number of Tourists to Antarctica Should Be Limited

Juan Kratzmaier

In the following viewpoint, Juan Kratzmaier argues that Antarctica must be protected from the impact of tourism. He applauds the work of the International Association of Antarctic Tour Operators (IAATO) and their self-imposed regulations. He argues, however, that because not all operators belong to the organization, there is no limit to the number of tourists who might visit Antarctica. He contends that tourism is a positive force, but that the numbers of tourists who can visit in a year should be limited by the Antarctic Treaty System countries. Kratzmaier is a travel photographer based in Barcelona, Spain.

As you read, consider the following questions:

1. Where are most tourist visits to Antarctica made, and why do tourists go there, according to Kratzmaier?

2. Who was the first promoter of tourism in Antarctica, according to the author?

Juan Kratzmaier, "Antarctica Tourism at the Limit?" *Institute of Marine Sciences*, February 2008. Reproduced by permission of the author.

3. As reported in the viewpoint, what is the ratio of guides to visitors under IAATO rules, and how does the rule affect the safety of the wildlife and the experience of the tourists?

The 2007/2008 tourist season will draw to a close in the middle of March. By then 47,000 more people will be able to say they have seen the *Terra Australis Incognita* [Latin for southern unknown land] with their own eyes.

A great commercial success for many, the Antarctic tourist industry is being questioned by many official bodies, environmental organisations and, behind the scenes, by the tourism companies themselves. It is the penguin that lays the golden eggs—but are we putting too much pressure on it?

In summer, when most of the sea ice has retreated, the surface area of the Antarctic is 14 million square kilometres, one and a half times the size of the Unites States of America. Nevertheless, 97% of tourist visits are made to the tip of the Antarctic Peninsula and the neighbouring South Shetland Islands (63° S, 59° W), a 1000 km coastline, with 200 or so places where it is possible to land. This is principally because this is the most temperate zone of the Antarctic, where there are most areas free of ice, more fauna, and more scientific bases, and it is the nearest point to a port, the world's most southern city, Ushuaia, on Tierra del Fuego, Argentina.

A Fragile Environment

It seems ridiculous that as few as 50,000 visitors could affect the environment of an entire continent, and in fact this isn't quite the case. However, this is an extremely fragile environment, and the risks of contaminating it must be minimised at all costs.

Studies carried out by the British Antarctic Survey and the National Science Foundation, the UK's [United Kingdom's] and USA's scientific bodies in the Antarctic, have regarded the impact of tourism benevolently, and, up to now, have not demonstrated that tourism has left any permanent or significant mark on the Antarctic territories, despite the number of visitors landing there having increased from 10,000 in 98/99 to 35,000 this season.

Nowadays, it is not so exotic to talk of having seen Cape Horn and sailed in the world's most notorious seas, the mythical Drake Passage that separates South America from Antarctica, a thousand kilometres of tales of storms and the wrecks of whalers and historic expeditionary ships.

But this is not just history. 2007 was an exceptional year, sounding a warning in this respect. A number of tourist ships got into difficulties, and two of these caused some environmental damage when they lost fuel. A spill from the *Nordkapp* discharged a small amount of marine diesel into the crater of Deception Island, while the *Explorer* sank in the Bransfield Strait with 190 tonnes of the same fuel on board.

A Responsible Model

Tourism in the Antarctic, thanks to its first promoter, Lars Eric Lindblad, and those who have followed in his footsteps, has always been an extremely responsible model, with a number of self-imposed measures intended to prevent the destruction or disturbance of the penguin that lays the golden eggs which we mentioned at the beginning of this article. In 1991, when tourism to the White Continent was already a reality, the seven companies operating at that time decided to form the IAATO (International Association of Antarctic Tour Operators), setting a worldwide example of how the private sector can regulate itself and establish rules of behaviour in a zone which lacks a regulating body.

About 95% of the companies working in the tourism sector below 60°S, around 100 companies, are members of IAATO. Its self-imposed regulations, generally strictly adhered to, include limits of the number of passengers that can land

The Growth of Antarctic Tourism

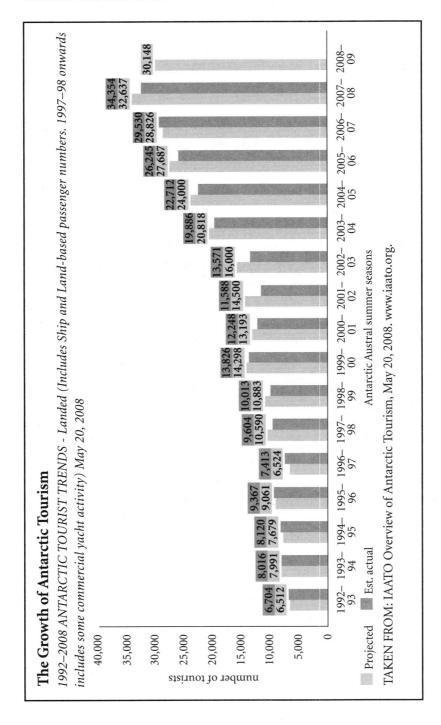

1992–2008 ANTARCTIC TOURIST TRENDS - Landed (Includes Ship and Land-based passenger numbers. 1997–98 onwards includes some commercial yacht activity) May 20, 2008

number of tourists

Antarctic Austral summer seasons

■ Projected ■ Est. actual

TAKEN FROM: IAATO Overview of Antarctic Tourism, May 20, 2008. www.iaato.org.

on any coastline (never more than 100 at a time), stipulating a minimum of 1 guide for every 20 visitors, and controlling the distance people must maintain between themselves and the wildlife (e.g. a minimum of 5 metres from nesting birds). These and dozens of other rules, covering everything from whale watching to walkable areas, combine with the environmental and navigating regulations for the Antarctic to keep the impact of tourist activities to the absolute minimum, in the most responsible way possible.

Some Companies Do Not Follow the Rules

Our present concerns are caused by companies that fail to respect the IAATO rules, by the intensive use of some landing sites, and by the lack of official regulations covering, for example, responsibilities in the event of rescues, evacuations, spills or any kind of accident. The number of ships is also cause for concern. In particular, enormous ships without reinforced hulls for sailing through ice, which use "heavy" fuels that are much less "digestible" by the ecosystem in the event of a spill, pose a serious ecological threat.

For these and other reasons, we must face up to the issues involved in a tourist industry which is responsible and positive, but which needs to be regulated and controlled more effectively before irreparable harm is done.

Tourism is an extremely positive force in Antarctica. The people who visit by cruise ship eat and sleep on the ship, minimising their impact on the environment. These people are accompanied throughout the trip by experts who teach them about geology, biology, history and conservation, ensuring that the majority return home with a greater environmental awareness, making them ambassadors for the Antarctic.

This should continue; people should be able to visit this wonderful place, but the moment has probably arrived to push for the creation by the signatories of the Antarctic Treaty of an official regulatory body. It needs to set a sensible limit

> *"Anyone, duly supervised, should be allowed to enjoy the wonders of polar regions, as of the world's deserts and forests."*

Polar Tourism Should Not Be Limited

Simon Jenkins

Simon Jenkins argues in the following viewpoint that tourists should be allowed to visit Antarctica, stating that scientists ought not be able to dictate who can or cannot come to the continent as a tourist. He asserts that it is ridiculous to allow only a few people "exclusive rights" to the polar regions. Further, he contends, the mineral wealth of the polar regions should likewise be shared among the people of the Earth. Jenkins is a journalist who writes for The Guardian, *a British newspaper.*

As you read, consider the following questions:

1. According to Jenkins, the centenaries of what two Antarctic landings were celebrated in 2008?

2. What is the name of an Antarctica tourist guide cited by Jenkins?

3. What does Jenkins have to say about the conservation of polar bears as an argument against mining in the Arctic?

Sitting on my desk is an illegal acquisition, a black pebble the size of a walnut. I picked it up some years ago on the slopes of Cape Crozier on Ross Island in the Antarctic. This vast wilderness of rock and ice lies on a cliff overlooking the Ross Sea and is celebrated as destination of the "worst journey in the world".

This was the title of the book written by Apsley Cherry-Garrard about a trip taken by him and two colleagues from [Robert Falcon] Scott's 1911 polar expedition to acquire the eggs of the Emperor penguin. The storm shelter of stones, canvas and bits of sledge from which they barely escaped alive still lies on the cape, literally frozen in time. I was visiting it with the doughty New Zealander David Harrowfield, recorder and conserver of the relics of mankind's earliest settlements on the Antarctic continent, including the vulnerable Scott and [Ernest] Shackleton huts.

A Breathtaking Vista

The spot must be one of the most breathtaking on earth, looking south over the Ross ice shelf towards the pole and north to the sweeping ocean icebergs. But it is forbidden to take anything from this land. No matter that removing my pebble had as much ecological impact as taking a grain of sand from the Sahara. The rulers of the greatest nanny state on earth, Antarctica, had declared it their own and only they can remove bits of it. I await the arrival of the Antarctic police, handcuffs at the ready.

We are in the midst of a flurry of centenaries of the heroic age of Antarctic exploration. One is of Shackleton's landing at Cape Royds and another, in three years, is of Scott's last, fatal voyage on the Terra Nova. Meanwhile, a combination of global warming and soaring raw material prices has seen a sudden revival of 50-year-old territorial aggrandisement, straining the agreements that govern the status of the polar regions.

Russia has claimed the mineral rights to the sea bed under the north pole. America is impeding conservation agreements so as to press ahead with its Alaskan oil and gas exploration. Britain is celebrating the centenary of its first claim to Antarctica by demanding a million square kilometres of the south Atlantic ocean bed. This is under the UN [United Nations] law of the sea convention, based on adjacent territorial claims in Antarctica.

Tourism has quadrupled in the past decade and continues to accelerate, despite the sinking last November of a cruise ship that hit an iceberg. Numbers rose last year alone by 14% to 37,000, almost all by ship. Tourists are banned from staying ashore and are strictly regulated as to what they can and cannot do.

A Double Standard

They are hated by scientists who "won" the continent under the 1959 Antarctic Treaty and are reluctant to relinquish it or share it with others. Annual Antarctic conferences yield such headlines as "Tourism threat to earth's last great wilderness". Scientists apparently pose no threat.

This double standard is well illustrated in the admirable *Lonely Planet* guide to Antarctica. A furious diktat against tourists picking up rocks or even feathers is carried alongside a scientist boasting the riches he has garnered from the place: "The problem is not in finding the fossils but in deciding which ones to collect."

The 1959 treaty is regularly proclaimed as a rare success of world government, albeit one protected by geographical vastness and climatic ferocity. It has held while everyone turned a blind eye to the Americans, who agreed to abide by it as long as they could do what they liked, including build bases at the poles. They are now constructing a 1,000-mile ice highway

Antarctic Tourism Can Be Environmentally Safe

"To date, private sector Antarctic tourism has developed as a remarkably low impact and cooperative model," [Executive Director of the International Association of Antarctic Tourism Operators (IAATO) Denise] Landau said in a statement at the meeting in Edinburgh. "Thousands of people have been able to experience and appreciate the Antarctic wilderness, with much less environmental impact than in any other part of the globe."

The IAATO has established procedures and guidelines for trips. They include regulations and restrictions on how many people can go ashore at one time, staff-to-passenger ratios and guidelines for activities while ashore. Procedures set up by the group also call for reporting both before and after visits.

Brian Witte,
"Calls for regulation of rising Antarctica tourism,"
The America's Intelligence Wire, *August 24, 2006.*

from McMurdo Station to the south pole. A brown cloud of pollution hovers off the Ross Shelf air base, where not just Hercules transport planes but Globemaster military jets are now able to land.

I can eulogise with the most florid romantic about the virgin wastes of ice, but I cannot see why nobody should be allowed to visit polar regions except scientists and eccentric explorers. The north and south ice caps are manifestly thawing and this is making both exploitation and tourism more feasible. The idea that a few lucky people should have exclusive rights to a mass of the world's surface is bizarre. It also leads to duplication and ridiculous national rivalry, such as India's building of a third base to prove that it is geologically part of Antarctica.

The Mineral Wealth of the Polar Regions Should Be Shared

Energy conservation may be a global imperative but to deny the peoples of the earth the mineral wealth of the Arctic regions is perverse. Aluminium, diamonds and even gold have been found in Greenland, so much so that the country is contemplating a return to the warm summers of the ninth century and independence of Denmark. Oil, gas and coal abound. If they are economic and their extraction can be governed by suitable environmental protocols—as is scientific research—what is the problem?

There is no reason why millions should go cold or hungry because some people like the idea of somewhere on Earth being pristine—or a private research laboratory. The conservation of the polar bear is a worthy cause, but like lions and elephants they can cohabit with man. To use their cause to forbid mineral extraction in the Arctic is as silly as it would be to plead the Emperor penguin as a reason for banning scientists from the Antarctic.

Tourists Should Be Allowed to Visit Antarctica

The condemnation of tourists for daring to encroach on these wonderful landscapes is equally unacceptable. These are not destinations for the masses. They are too distant and costly, and tolerable only in summer. But anyone, duly supervised, should be allowed to enjoy the wonders of polar regions, as of the world's deserts and forests. Ice is ecologically fragile, but these lands are vast. Besides, the best ambassadors for polar conservation are those who pay good money to see it.

An apocalyptic report this week from Brussels bewailed a northwards migration of mankind as the ice caps melt and the tropics become less inhabitable. This is surely a natural balancing of the occupants of planet earth in response to climate change. The mining settlements round the Arctic Circle, the tourists on the Antarctic peninsula and the American base at McMurdo Station are not going to shrink.

What is clear is that some new governing framework must be developed to meet these changes, wider in accountability than to Big Science. There is no way national self-interest will be kept at bay unless a stronger body is granted sovereign authority, presumably under the United Nations.

Scientists and soldiers simply cannot tell tourists and prospectors to get lost from a chunk of the planet. The beauties and the riches of these regions are increasingly accessible and must be governed for the benefit of all, as should be the skies and the oceans. They are paradises made in hell, but they are no longer unknowable or untouchable. Those days are over.

Periodical Bibliography

The following articles have been selected to supplement the diverse views presented in this chapter.

Elizabeth Bluemink	"Remote Alaska Communities Become Winter Tourism Destinations," *Anchorage Daily News*, January 24, 2008.
British Antarctic Survey	"Antarctic Tourism," 2007. www.Antarctica.ac.uk.
Leo Hickman	"To Coldly Go: Tourism Is Encroaching on Antarctica," *The Guardian*, June 6, 2008. www.guardian.co.uk.
Anne Kalosh	"Beyond 'The World's Most Beautiful Voyage,'" *Vacation Agent Magazine*, September 1, 2006. www.travelpulse.com.
Nick Nuttall	"Rapid Rise in Tourism New Challenge to Polar Environment," *State News Service*, June 3, 2007.
Ricardo Roura	"The Case Against Tourism Landings from Ships Carrying More than 500 Passengers," Antarctic Treaty Consultative Meeting, May 11, 2007.
Emma J. Stewart, S.E.L. Howard, D. Draper et al.	"Sea Ice in Canada's Arctic: Implications for Cruise Tourism," *Arctic*, vol. 60, no. 4, December 2007.
Oliver Tickel	"Tourism Threatens Antarctica," *Times Online*, June 5, 2007. www.timesonline.co.uk.
Lew Toulmin	"Tragedy Fuels Debate Re Antarctic Cruising," *International Travel News*, vol. 30, no. 11, January 2006.
Bob Weber	"Record Number of Cruise Ships in Canadian Arctic This Summer," *The Canadian Press*, August 17, 2008. http://cnews.canoe.ca.

For Further Discussion

Chapter 1

1. The viewpoints in this chapter offer several perspectives regarding governance of the polar regions. What country or countries do you think has the strongest territorial claims in the Arctic? In the Antarctic? Explain your answers using examples from the viewpoints.

2. What do you think the role of indigenous peoples should be in the governance of the Arctic?

3. After reading the viewpoints in this chapter, and reading the text of the Antarctic Treaty (easily accessed on the Internet), do you think the Antarctic Treaty System (ATS) is an effective governing agreement for Antarctica? Why or why not?

4. Should a system similar to the ATS be developed for the Arctic? Why or why not?

Chapter 2

1. According to the viewpoints in this chapter, what are the biggest threats to the polar regions from climate change?

2. Colin Woodard believes melting polar ice will cause ocean levels to rise rapidly. Jerome J. Schmitt disagrees. Which argument do you find most convincing? Why?

3. Several writers in this chapter discuss the effects of climate change on the people and wildlife of the Arctic region. What changes will the people and animals of the Arctic have to make to adjust to the changing climate? How successful do you believe they will be in making the transition? Explain your answers using evidence from the viewpoints.

4. What are some of the beneficial consequences of climate change in the polar regions as cited in the viewpoints of this chapter? How do these weigh against the negative consequences projected?

Chapter 3

1. What are some of the natural resources that could be developed in the polar regions, according to the viewpoints in this chapter? Who should benefit financially from the development of natural resources in the polar regions, and why?

2. Which do you find more convincing: the arguments for preservation of the polar regions or the arguments for the development of natural resources? Explain your answers using examples from the viewpoints.

3. Felix von Geyer and Simon Handelsman argue that polar indigenous peoples could benefit from the development of natural resources in the Arctic. Macdonald Stainsby disagrees. Do you think indigenous peoples would be helped or harmed by resource development in the Arctic? Explain your answers using examples from the viewpoints.

Chapter 4

1. Why do you think that so many people want to travel to the far north and the far south?

2. How do you think tourism could contribute to the protection of the polar regions? How could tourism harm the polar regions? Using examples from the viewpoints, explain whether you think tourism should be limited.

3. If tourism to the polar regions were to be limited by law, how do you think the decision should be made as to who can visit?

4. Based on the arguments presented in the viewpoints, do you think polar cruise travel is safe and adequately regulated? Give examples from the viewpoints to support your answer.

Organizations to Contact

The editors have compiled the following list of organizations concerned with the issues debated in this book. The descriptions are derived from materials provided by the organizations. All have publications or information available for interested readers. The list was compiled on the date of publication of the present volume; the information provided here may change. Be aware that many organizations take several weeks or longer to respond to inquiries, so allow as much time as possible.

Australian Antarctic Division
Channel Highway, Kingston, Australia, Tasmania
  7050
+61 3 6232 3209 • fax: +61 3 6232 3288
e-mail: Available as link through Web site
Web site: www.aad.au

The Australian Antarctic Division is the Australian governmental agency responsible for administering and maintaining Australia's interests in Antarctica and also works to support the Antarctic Treaty System. The organization offers a searchable database of publications on its Web site, including *ANARE Reports*, which summarize the work of the Australian National Antarctic Research Expeditions. The Web site includes an extensive illustrated set of related articles describing living and working in Antarctica.

British Antarctic Survey (BAS)
High Cross, Madingley Road, Cambridge, United Kingdom
  CB3 OET
+44 0 1223 221400 • fax: +44 0 1223 362616
Web site: www.Antarctica.ac.uk

The BAS is responsible for conducting research in and around Antarctica. The organization's Web site not only contains descriptions of the BAS research, it also includes fact sheets about Antarctica, full-text news articles, and a chart showing current temperatures at seven research stations and aboard two vessels in Antarctica. Science articles, such as "Frozen in Time: Fossils from Antarctica," and "Polar Science for Planet Earth," are appropriate for students and the general public.

Canadian Arctic Resources Committee (CARC)
488 Gladstone Ave., Ottawa, Canada   K1N 8VA
613-759-4284 • fax: 613-237-3845
e-mail: davidg@carc.org
Web site: www.carc.org

CARC is a citizen's advocacy organization that works for the "long-term environmental and social well-being of Northern Canada and its people." The group sponsors 2030 North, a Canadian National Planning Conference scheduled for June 2009. Information about and papers related to the conference appear on the Web site. In addition, CARC publishes *Northern Perspectives*, a magazine archived on the Web site.

Defenders of Wildlife
1130 17th St. NW, Washington, DC   20036
202-682-9400
e-mail: defenders@mail.defenders.org
Web site: www.defenders.org

Defenders of Wildlife is a science-based, nonprofit organization dedicated to wildlife conservation. On its Web site, the group publishes research studies and analyses of endangered wildlife, including polar bears and other Arctic and Antarctic flora and fauna, as well as news articles and fact sheets. In addition, Defenders of Wildlife publishes *Defender Magazine*, also available on the Web site.

International Association of Antarctica Tour Operators (IAATO)
11 S. Angell St., Box 302, Providence, RI   02906
401-272-2152 • fax: 401-272-2154

e-mail: iaato@iaato.org
Web site: www.iaato.org

The IAATO works to "promote and practice safe and environmentally responsible private-sector travel to the Antarctic," according to the group's Web site. Also on the Web site are statistics concerning tourism in the Antarctic and images of the region. The IAATO publishes the *IAATO Science News Sheet* in addition to other informative articles and links to other resources available on its Web site.

International Polar Foundation
Rue des Deux Gares/Tweetstationsstraat 120 A
Bruxelles/Brussels   B1070
   Belgium
+32 02 543 06 98 • fax: +32 02 543 0699
e-mail: info@polarfoundation.org
Web site: www.polarfoundation.org

The International Polar Foundation communicates with the public about issues related to polar science and research, and strives to educate people about the region. On its Web site, students will find pictures from webcams at the Poles as well as a monthly newsletter. In addition, the organization maintains three additional Web sites, all accessible from www.polarfoundation.org, or individually. SciencePoles (www.sciencepoles.org) offers scientific information. EducaPoles (www.educapoles.org) has a wide array of multimedia demonstrations and projects for students and educators alike. ExploraPoles (www.explorapoles.org) offers information about polar adventure and expeditions. Combined, the Web sites of the International Polar Foundation offer a wealth of information for those who want to know more about the North and South Poles.

International Polar Year (IPY)
IPY International Programme Office, c/o British Antarctic
   Survey, High Cross, Madingley Rd., Cambridge   CB3 OET
   United Kingdom

+44 0 1223 221 468 • fax: +44 0 1223 221 270
e-mail: ipyipo@bas.ac.uk
Web site: www.ipy.org

The International Polar Year is a large scientific program studying the northern and southern polar regions from 2007 through 2009. Sponsored by the International Council for Science and the World Meteorological Organization, the IPY encompasses more than 200 projects with scientists from more than 60 nations. The IPY Web site includes research results, maps, charts, a multimedia presentation of Students on Ice (the journey of a group of university students traveling from the far north to the far south), archives of full text articles concerning the Arctic and Antarctic, and a range of blogs by scientists participating in studies.

Inuit Circumpolar Council (ICC)
ICC Greenland, Dronning Ingridsvej 1, PO Box 204
Nuuk   DK-3900
  Greenland
299 323632 • fax: 299 323001
e-mail: iccgreenland@inuit.org
Web site: www.inuit.org

The Inuit Circumpolar Council is the international organization representing Inuit peoples living across the far north of Alaska, Canada, Greenland, and Russia. The organization's goals and activities include promoting Inuit and worldwide indigenous rights, developing and preserving Inuit Culture, and working to preserve the environment. ICC's Web site includes reports from working groups and commissions, news articles, and information concerning Inuit culture and education.

Inuit Tapiriit Kanatami (ITK)
75 Albert St., Suite 1101, Ottawa, Ontario   K1P 5E7
  Canada
613-238-8181 • fax: 613-234-1991

e-mail: info@itk.ca
Web site: www.itk.ca

Inuit Tapiriit Kanatami, is a large national organization representing Canada's Inuit population. The organization's Web site holds a wealth of information regarding Inuit culture, land, peoples, and rights, as well as a history of the Inuit people and the creation of Nunavut, the largest and newest territory of Canada. ITK publishes *Inuktitut Magazine* in both Inuktitut and English; back issues of the magazine are available on the Web site.

Japan Whaling Association (JWA)
Toyomishinko Building 7F, 4-5 Toyomi-cho
Chuoah-ku Tokyo
e-mail: kujira@whaling.jp
Web site: www.whaling.jp

The Japan Whaling Association communicates with the public about Japanese policies concerning whaling. It is a useful source for students wishing to examine the dispute between Australia and Japan over whaling in Antarctic waters from the Japanese perspective. The group publishes the *JWA Newsletter*, as well as other informative articles, including "Why Whale Research?" The Web site also includes an extensive Q&A section, a history of whaling, and many news articles.

National Science Foundation, Office of Polar Programs
4201 Wilson Blvd., Arlington, VA 22230
703-292-5111
e-mail: info@nsf.gov
Web site: www.nsf.gov/od/opp

The Office of Polar Programs of the National Science Foundation manages and initiates research at both poles. Its projects focus on understanding the Earth and its systems; exploring the geographical frontier; and performing science enabled by the polar setting. Publications include the *Antarctic Sun* newspaper.

United Nations Environment Programme/GRID-Arendal
Postboks 183, Arendal   N-4802
  Norway
+47 47 64 45 55 • fax: +47 37 03 50 50
e-mail: grid@grida.no
Web site: www.grida.no

The United Nations Environment Programme (UNEP)/GRID-Arendal is a collaborative center that manages and assesses environmental information, as well as providing communication and outreach to all the countries of the world. Students can access materials from the UNEP Polar Program through the GRID-Arendal Web site. In addition, the organization offers maps, graphics, news articles, and publications about climate change and the polar regions.

Bibliography of Books

Frances Abele, Thomas J. Courchene, F. Leslie Seidle, et. al., eds. — *Northern Exposures: Peoples, Powers, and Prospects for Canada's North.* Montreal: Institute for Research on Public Policy, 2008.

Roberto Bargali — *Antarctic Ecosystems: Environmental Contamination, Climate Change, and Human Impact.* New York: Springer, 2006.

Arnoldus Schytte Blix — *Arctic Animals and Their Adaptations to Life on the Edge.* Trondheim, Norway: Tapir Academic Press, 2005.

Marla Cone — *Silent Snow: The Slow Poisoning of the Arctic.* New York: Grove Press, 2005.

Sebastian Copeland — *Antarctica: The Global Warming.* San Rafael, CA: Earth Aware, 2007.

David Crane — *Scott of the Antarctic: A Life of Courage and Tragedy.* New York: Knopf, 2006.

Felipe Fernández-Armesto — *Pathfinders: A Global History of Exploration.* New York: W.W. Norton, 2006.

William L. Fox — *Terra Antarctica: Looking into the Emptiest Continent.* San Antonio, TX: Trinity University Press, 2005.

Tom Griffiths   *Slicing the Silence: Voyaging to Antarctica*. Cambridge, MA: Harvard University Press, 2007.

Bruce Henderson   *True North: Peary, Cook, and the Race to the Pole*. New York: W.W. Norton, 2005.

Mike Horn   *Conquering the Impossible: My 12,000-mile Journey around the Arctic Circle*. New York: St. Martin's Press, 2007.

Robert Jarvenpa and Hetty Jo Brumbach   *Circumpolar Lives and Livelihood: A Comparative Ethnoarchaeology of Gender and Subsistence*. University of Nebraska Press, 2006.

Roger Kaye   *Last Great Wilderness: The Campaign to Establish the Arctic National Wildlife Refuge*. Fairbanks, AK: University of Alaska Press, 2006.

David A. Kearns   *Where Hell Freezes Over: A Story of Amazing Bravery and Survival*. New York: Thomas Dunne Books, 2005.

Elizabeth Kolbert, ed.   *Field Notes from a Catastrophe: Man, Nature, and Climate Change*. New York: Bloomsbury Publishers, 2006.

Elizabeth Kolbert, ed   *The Ends of the Earth: An Anthology of the Finest Writing on the Arctic and the Antarctic*. New York: Bloomsbury USA, 2007.

Gretchen Legler   *On the Ice: An Intimate Portrait of Life in McMurdo Station, Antarctica.* Minneapolis: Milkweed Editions, 2005.

Michael C. MacCracken and Frances Moore   *Sudden and Disruptive Climate Change: Exploring the Real Risks and How We Can Avoid Them.* Sterling, VA: Earthscan, 2008.

Robert McGhee   *The Last Imaginary Place: A Human History of the Arctic.* New York: Oxford University Press, 2005.

David McGonigal   *Antarctica: Secrets of the Southern Continent.* Richmond Hill, Ontario: Firefly Books, 2008.

Melanie McGrath   *The Long Exile: A Tale of Inuit Betrayal and Survival in the High Arctic.* New York: Knopf, 2007.

Sarah Moss   *The Frozen Ship: The Histories and Tales of Polar Exploration.* New York: Bluebridge, 2006.

Dieter K. Müller   *Tourism in the Peripheries: Perspectives from the Far North and South.* Cambridge, MA: CABI, 2007.

Markm Nuttall   *Encyclopedia of the Arctic.* New York: Routledge, 2005.

Greg O'Hare, John Sweeney, and Rob Wilby   *Weather, Climate, and Climate Change: Human Perspectives.* New York: Pearson Prentice Hall, 2005.

Fred Pearce

With Speed and Violence: Why Scientists Fear Tipping Points in Climate Change. Boston: Beacon, 2007.

Beau Riffenburgh

Encyclopedia of the Antarctic. New York: Routledge, 2008.

Leslie Carol Roberts

The Entire Earth and Sky: Views on Antarctica. Lincoln, NE: University of Nebraska Press, 2008.

Lisle Abbot Rose

Explorer: The Life of Richard E. Byrd. Columbia, MO: University of Missouri Press, 2008.

Norbert Rosing

The World of the Polar Bear. Richmond Hill, Ontario: Firefly Books, 2006.

Hadoram Shirihai

The Complete Guide to Antarctic Wildlife: Birds and Marine Mammals of the Antarctic Continent and the Southern Ocean. Princeton, NJ: Princeton University Press, 2008.

Roff Martin Smith

Life on the Ice: No One Goes to Antarctica Alone. Washington, DC: National Geographic, 2005.

J. Snyder and Bernard Stonehouse

Prospects for Polar Tourism. Cambridge, MA: CABI, 2007.

J. Snyder and Bernard Stonehouse

Tourism in the Polar Regions: The Sustainability Challenge. Washington DC: The International Ecotourism Society, 2007.

Michael A.
Sommers

*Antarctic Melting: The Disappearing
Antarctic Ice Cap*. New York: Rosen
Group, 2007.

David M.
Standlea

*Oil, Globalization, and the War for
the Arctic Refuge*. Albany, NY: State
University of New York Press, 2006.

David N. Thomas
and G.E. Fogg

The Biology of Polar Regions. New
York: Oxford University Press, 2008.

Index

A

Aboriginal peoples, 79, 144–146
Aboriginal Pipeline Group, 153–154
Adaptation concerns
    Arctic protection/management, 134, 136
    climate change, 102, 105–112
    greenhouse gas effect, 87
    of indigenous peoples, 103, 105–106, 111–112
    of polar bears, 122, 125
"Adventure tourism," 175
Agreement for Cooperation relating to the Marine Environment (Canada-Denmark), 83
Alaska
    coastal expansion, 60–61, 78
    indigenous peoples of, 19
    oil in, 20, 158–159, 193
    polar bear extinction in, 117, 124, 133
    polar thaw in, 92–93
    sea ice loss in, 116, 123
    shipping control by, 84
Alaska Native Claims Settlement Act, 146
Alaskan Department of Natural Resources, 93
Alexie, Roberta A., 154
Amundsen, Roald, 16–17
Antarctic
    British Antarctic Survey, 29–37
    environmental protection in, 28, 36–37, 39, 53
    future of, 53–54
    governance of, 29–37, 38–44, 45–55
    history of, 46–48
    political regime of, 175
    sea ice loss in, 58, 90
    South Pole expeditions, 16–17
    sovereignty in, 26, 34, 39–44, 43
    tourist regulation in, 173–177, 178–184
    travel dangers in, 171
    weather of, 30–31
Antarctic, territorial claims on
    establishing sovereignty, 26
    future conflicts, 26–28
    overlapping claims, 23–25
    by U.K., 23, 26–27
    See also Antarctic Treaty System
Antarctic and Southern Ocean Coalition (ASOC), 37, 173–177
Antarctic Minerals Convention, 130
Antarctic Treaty Consultive Meeting (ATCM), 35
Antarctic Treaty System (ATS)
    as Arctic treaty model, 64–65
    articles/aims of, 33–34, 47–48
    background of, 40–41
    conflict prevention and, 24
    defects in, 40, 50, 52–53
    enforcement weakness of, 41–42
    environmental protection and, 41, 43, 48–51
    future of, 53–54

governance under, 19, 39, 43–
44, 54–55
Madrid Protocol and, 26, 48–
49, 52, 130–131
members of, 31–34
political cooperation with, 51
specialized bodies of, 36–37
success record of, 34–36, 41
tourist regulations and, 49–50,
176–177, 183
*Antarctica and South American
Geopolitics* (Child), 27
Antarctica Tourism Campaign,
174, 177
Anti-drilling factions, 160
Arctic
biodiversity protection in,
134–136
environmental protection of,
61–62, 68
ice cap and, 57–58
joint control of, 80–84
mapping floor of, 139, 141
national security and, 137–
142, 167
natural resource protection of,
132–136
oil drilling in, 163–164
sea ice warming, 91–92
warming, 122–124
See also Gas pipelines; Indigenous peoples
Arctic, territorial claims on
Canadian, 70–79
military equipment and,
59–60
positioning strategies for,
61–62
proving of, 58
Russian strategy for, 57–58
shipping lanes and, 81–83

U.S. position on, 60–61, 138
See also Arctic treaty
Arctic Climate Impact Assessment
(ACIA) report, 112, 123–124
Arctic Council, 20, 62, 68–69, 109
Arctic Dreams (Lopez), 15
Arctic Environmental Protection
Strategy, 68
Arctic National Wildlife Refuge
(ANWR), 142, 158–162, 163–166
Arctic treaty
Arctic Council role in, 68–69
challenges to, 69
draft proposal for, 66–68
Norway claims and, 65–66
vs. Antarctic treaty, 64–65
Arctic Waters Pollution Prevention
Act (AWPPA), 75, 82, 84
"Are Sunspots Prime Suspects in
Global Warming" (Spotts), 88
Argentina, 24, 26–27, 180
Argentine Antarctic Institute, 90
Australia, 49, 53, 130

B

Baldacchino, Geoffrey, 171
Ban Ki Moon, 27–28
Barkham, Patrick, 170
Bathurst Inlet port development,
145–146
Beaufort Sea dispute, 61, 76, 78
Belkin, Janet, 45–55
Berger, Thomas R. (inquiry), 151–
152
Biodiversity in Arctic, 134–136
"Bioprospecting," 49
Bone, James, 22–28
Borgerson, Scott, 59

British Antarctic Survey, 29–37, 186

Brooks, Arthur E., 59

Burnett, H. Sterling, 121–126

Bush, George W. (administration), 114, 119–120, 163–164

C

Cabot, John, 14

Canada

    indigenous peoples in, 103, 150

    mining, 145

    natural resources, 141–142

    polar thaw and, 92–93

Canada, territorial claims by

    Arctic Council and, 68, 109

    Arctic waters control by, 80–84

    Beaufort Sea dispute, 61, 76, 78

    continental shelf and, 58, 74–75, 79

    Denmark and, 80–84

    environmental protection authority and, 75, 79

    Hans Island case, 72, 78

    indigenous peoples and, 19

    internal waters and, 73–74

    land claims, 58–61

    legal basis for, 71–72

    maritime claims, 72–73, 75

    Northwest Passage dispute, 20, 61, 76, 77, 78–79

    shipping lanes and, 81–83

    Svalbard Treaty, 65

    transit fees, 84

    trilateral agreement with, 83–84

    twelve-mile territorial sea limit, 72–74

    U.S. and, 77, 80–84, 141–142

Capper, Linda, 26

Casassa, Gino, 26–27

Center for Biological Diversity, 122

Child, Jack, 27

Chile, 23–27, 50, 180, 183

Christy, John R., 88

Chukchi Sea, 115, 117–120, 123

Clark, Jamie Rappaport, 113–120

Climate change

    adaptation concerns, 102, 105–112

    cosmic ray influence, 88

    economic development and, 64, 109

    indigenous peoples adapted to, 107–112

    indigenous peoples threatened by, 101–106

    mining and, 130

    Northwest Passage and, 77

    oil drilling and, 27

    polar bears endangered by, 113–120

    polar bears not endangered by, 121–126

    poles affected by, 133, 144, 147–148

    regional tension over, 59, 64

    resource management and, 79

    sun spots, 88

    thinning glaciers, 91

    tourism and, 170, 196

    See also Global warming; Polar ice melt

Climate Science: Climate Change and Its Impacts (Legates), 122

Clinton, Bill (administration), 158

Coast Guard (U.S.), 82, 141
Cohen, Ariel, 137–142
Collett, Tim, 147
Congressional Research Service, 160
Connor, Steve, 88
Conservation concerns
    Antarctic Treaty System and, 35, 36
    Arctic Treaty and, 66
    biodiversity protection, 134–136
    fossil fuels, 118–120
    for natural resources, 133–134
    organizations, 37–38
    See also Climate change; Environmental protection; Global warming; Oil drilling; Polar bears; Polar ice melt; Tourism
Convention on the Law of the Sea (UNCLOS)
    Antarctica Treaty System and, 54
    Arctic Waters Pollution Prevention Act and, 84
    maritime claims and, 72
    Russia and, 139
    territorial claims and, 58, 73–74
Cook, Frederick A., 16
Corell, Robert, 92–93
Cosmic ray influence, 88
Côté, François, 70–79
Council of Managers of National Antarctic Programs (COMNSAP), 36
Cowing, Charles, 15

D

Deh Cho (Dene) nation, 154–155
DeMille, Dianne, 80–84
Denmark
    Arctic Council and, 68, 109
    Arctic waters control by, 80–84
    Greenland independence from, 144, 195
    Hans Island and, 60, 72, 78
    indigenous peoples and, 19
    shipping lanes and, 81–83
    shoreline claims by, 58
    Svalbard Treaty and, 65–66
    transit fees, 84
    trilateral agreement with, 83–84
Department of Fisheries and Oceans (Canada) study, 124
Department of Indian Affairs, 155
Department of Interior, 116
Diavik diamond mine, 144–145
Dolbow, Jim, 137–142
Draper, D., 171
Driessen, Paul, 157–161
Dufresne, Robert, 70–79

E

Economic development
    Arctic Treaty and, 67, 69
    biodiversity and, 134–135
    climate change and, 64, 109
    Diavik diamond mine, 144–145
    exclusive economic zone and, 58, 61, 74–75
    gas pipelines and, 150–151, 153–155
    globalization and, 42, 44, 51, 103, 133

of hydrocarbons, 138–139
of indigenous peoples, 102–
  104, 106, 145–146, 152
of mineral wealth, 138
Northwest Passage and, 20
political cooperation over, 51
by U.S., 141–142
See also Oil drilling
Eduardo Frei Montalva Air Force
  Base (Chile), 23–24
Eilperin, Juliet, 88
Eisenhower, Dwight D., 129
Endangered Species Act, 114, 117,
  120
Energy Information Administration (EIA), 165, 166
Environmental Impact Assessment, 175, 182
Environmental protection
  by Antarctic Treaty System,
    41, 43, 48–51
  in Antarctica, 28, 36–37, 39,
    53
  anti-drilling factions and, 160
  of Arctic, 61–62, 68
  by Canada, 75
  natural resources and, 134–
    136, 150–152
  tar sands extraction and, 156
  vs. tourism, 170, 181–182,
    186–187, 194
  See also Adaptation concerns;
    Climate change; Conserva-
    tion concerns; Natural re-
    sources
Eurasian continental shelf, 58
Exclusive Economic Zone, 58, 74–
  75, 139
Explorer (cruise ship), 46, 54, 171,
  187

Extinction concerns. *See* Polar
  bears
"Extreme tourism," 170–172
*Extreme Tourism: Lessons from the
  World's Cold Water Islands*
  (Baldacchino), 171

F

Fish and Wildlife Service
  (USFWS), 122
"Fly-sail" operations, 175
Flynn, Sian, 16
Fossil fuels, 46, 114, 118–120,
  150–151
Franklin, John, 15

G

Gas pipelines
  development of, 26, 138, 160,
    164, 193
  economic development and,
    150–151, 153–155
  indigenous peoples and, 149–
    156
  MacKenzie Gas Project, 150–
    151, 153–155
  polar bears and, 114–115,
    117–118, 120
  polar ice melt and, 93, 109
  territorial claim over, 58, 138
  tourism and, 133, 195
Geological Survey (U.S.), 58, 117,
  160, 167
Global warming
  Arctic ice cap and, 57–58
  calculating, 96–97
  Ice-free summer seas, 145
  mineral resources and, 26
  momentum of, 87–88, 93
  polar bears and, 124–126

shipping lanes and, 57
territorial claims and, 23, 192
See also Climate change; Polar
ice melt
Globalization, 42, 44, 51, 103, 133
Gore, Al, 95, 98, 100
"A Green Tipping Point" (Walsh),
87
Greenhouse gas effect
adaptation concerns, 87
Mackenzie Gas Project and,
151
on polar bears, 117, 118, 120
on polar ice melt, 92, 95, 124
Greenland, 19, 58, 93, 144
Greenpeace organization, 122, 130
Griffiths, Franklyn, 82

H

Handelsman, Simon, 143–148
Hans Island dispute, 60, 72, 78
Harper, Stephen, 59, 60–61, 75,
147
Harrowfield, David, 192
Hazlett, Sue, 132–136
Henson, Matthew A., 15–16
Herber, Bernard P., 51
Herschel, William, 88
Hoefer, Tom, 145
Holubec, Igor, 147
Huettmann, Falk, 132–136
Hybrid cars, 167
Hydroelectric resources, 160

I

IAATO. *See* International Association of Antarctic Tour Operators
Ice caps/melt. *See* Polar ice melt

Indigenous peoples
aboriginal, 79, 144–146
adaptation strategies of, 103,
105–106, 111–112
Arctic development and, 137–
142
benefits to, 145–146
challenges/opportunities of,
109–110, 147–148
climate change impact, 104–
106, 108–109
Deh Cho (Dene) nation, 154–
155
demographics of, 19–20
development harm to, 68–69,
149–156
economic development of,
102–104, 106, 145–146, 152
importance of, 102–103
Inupiat, 153
MacKenzie Gas Project, 150–
151, 153–155
natural resources and, 134–
136, 143–148
Norse peoples, 14
oil drilling and, 153
Sami peoples, 144
traditional knowledge of, 112
See also Inuit peoples
Inter-American Commission on
Human Rights (IACHR), 105
Intergovernmental Oceanographic
Commission, 37
Intergovernmental Panel on Climate Change, 91
Internal waters, 72–73
International Association of Antarctic Tour Operators (IAATO)
Antarctic Treaty System and,
37, 49–50, 54–55
role of, 183–184
tourist safety by, 171, 194

International Court of Justice (ICJ), 44

International Geophysical Year (IGY), 31, 47, 57, 129

International Hydrographic Organisation, 37

International Maritime Organization, 55

International Polar Year, 42, 87, 133, 136

International Union for the Conservation of Nature (IUCN), 36, 134

Inuit Circumpolar Conference, 93

Inuit peoples
  adaptive capacity of, 14–15, 110
  climate change and, 104, 105
  demographics of, 19
  ice melt impact on, 92–93
  industry vs. government partnerships with, 146–147
  oil drilling and, 153, 159

Inupiat peoples, 153

J

Japanese fishermen, 50

Jenkins, Simon, 191–196

Jones, Barnaby, 52–53

K

Kane, Elisha Kent, 15

Koiurova, Timo, 101–106

Kratzmaier, Juan, 185–190

Krill hunting, 50

Kyoto treaty, 151

L

Larsen ice shelf, 90

Latent heat, 99–100

Laviolette, Tom, 155

Lee, Martin Lishexian, 38–44

Legates, David, 122–123

Lindblad, Lars Eric, 187

Lomonosov Ridge, 58

Lopez, Barry, 15

M

Macchi, Mirjam, 107–112

MacKay, Peter, 57

MacKenzie Gas Project, 150–151, 153–155

MacKenzie Valley Environmental Impact Review Board, 151, 154

Madrid Protocol, 26, 48–49, 52, 130–131

Malaysia, 28, 55

Minerals Management Service (MMS), 116–117

Mining/mineral resources
  climate change and, 130, 144–145, 196
  Madrid Protocol and, 48, 130
  outlawing, 26
  territorial conflicts over, 40, 43
  See also Gas pipelines; Oil drilling

Morgan, Barbara, 146

Murmansk Shipping Company, 60

N

National Center for Policy Analysis (NCPA), 122

National Science Foundation, 186

National security (U.S.)
  Arctic development and, 137–142, 167
  indigenous peoples and, 149–156
  protection of, 132–136
  Russian ambitions and, 139–140
  U.S. presence in Arctic, 139–142
  See also Oil drilling
National Snow and Ice Data Center (U.S.), 115
Natural Resources Defense Council (NRDC), 162–167
New Zealand, 130, 176, 179, 183
Norse peoples, 14
North American Aerospace Defense Command (NORAD), 82
North Pole, 15–16, 57, 193
Northern Development and Imperial Oil, 155
Northern Sea Route, 138
Northwest Passage
  Canadian claims to, 20, 61, 76, 77, 78–79
  climate change and, 77
  importance of, 20
  navigation of, 14, 16, 138
  as shipping lanes, 81–83
  territorial dispute over, 60–61, 73, 75–79
  transit fees through, 84
  trilateral agreement over, 83–84
Norway
  Antarctic Treaty System and, 31, 33, 129
  Arctic Council and, 68
  indigenous groups in, 19, 109
  Svalbard Treaty and, 65–66
  territorial claims by, 58
  U.S. cooperation with, 141

O

Ocean levels. See Polar ice melt
Oceans Act, 74
Oil drilling
  in Alaska, 158–159
  as beneficial, 142, 160–161
  distraction vs. solution of, 165–166
  energy security and, 167
  environmental impact of, 117–118
  opposition to, 164–165
  reserves, 27
  as threat, 153
  vs. protecting Arctic, 163–164
Outer Continental Shelf (OCS), 139, 142, 162

P

Peary, Robert E., 15–16
Penguin population, 49–50
Peterson, Kim, 104
Pharand, Donat, 66
Polar bears
  adaptability of, 125
  Arctic warming and, 122–124
  extinction projections of, 117, 124
  fossil fuel reduction and, 118–120
  global warming and, 124–126
  oil/gas leasing harm to, 117–118
  polar ice melt and, 115–116, 124
  population status of, 119, 122, 125

protection of, 114–115, 133
sea ice loss and, 116–117
Polar ice melt
    Arctic warming and, 91–92
    climatologists and, 95–96
    coastal areas and, 93
    facts about, 98–99
    glacier thinning, 91
    greenhouse gas effect on, 95
    Inuit communities and, 92–93
    latent heat and, 99–100
    polar bears and, 115–116, 124
    sea level rising and, 98, 100
Priestley, Stephen, 147
Putin, Vladimir, 60

R

Rasmussen, Rasmus Ole, 63–69
Roper-Gee, Rebecca, 178–184
Rusling, Matthew, 59
Russia
    Arctic territory strategies of,
      48, 57–58, 60–61, 139–140
    bioprospecting by, 49
    coastal-station records, 123
    ice studies by, 123
    Northern sea route and, 138
    polar claims by, 20, 24, 57, 81,
      193
    U.S. diplomacy with, 141

S

Sack, Karen, 27
Sami indigenous peoples, 144
Scambos, Ted, 91
Schaefer, Jack, 153
Schmitt, Jerome J., 94–100
Scientific Committee on Antarctic
    Research (SCAR), 36
Scott, Robert Falcon, 16–17, 192

Sea ice loss and, 116–117, 124
Sea-level rise calculations, 98, 100
Security and Prosperity Partner-
    ship of North America, 82
Shackleton, Ernest, 16, 23, 192
Shadian, Jessica, 20
Skvarca, Pedro, 90
Soudas, Dimitri, 147
South America, 23, 47, 180
South Pole expeditions, 16–17
Spotts, Peter N., 88
Stainsby, Macdonald, 149–156
Stepien, Adam, 101–106
Steward, E.J., 171
Sun spots climate influence, 88
Svalbard Treaty, 65–66
Szaszdi, Lajos F., 137–142

T

Tar sands extraction, 156
Terra Nullius (nobody's land) con-
    cept, 64
Tervo, Henna, 101–106
Tourism
    in Antarctica, 173–177, 178–
      184
    "extreme tourism," 170
    growth of, 42, 109, 188
    history of, 174–175, 179, 192–
      193
    IAATO role in, 183–184
    impact of, 106, 181–182, 186–
      187
    mineral wealth and, 195
    regulating, 49–50, 175–177,
      182–183, 189–190
    responsible model of, 54–55,
      187–189
    ship-bourne, 180–181

support for, 195–196
"trophy tourists," 170
T'Seleie, Frank, 152

U

United Kingdom (U.K.)
    Antarctic, territorial claims by,
    23, 26–27
    Antarctic Treaty System and,
    31, 33, 129
    British Antarctic Survey and,
    29–37, 186
    oil drilling and, 52
    Svalbard Treaty and, 65
    territory claims by, 23–24,
    26–28, 71, 193
United Nations (UN)
    Antarctica governance by, 38–
    44, 45–55
    Commission on the Limits of
    the Continental Shelf, 58
    Environment Program, 37
    See also Convention on the
    Law of the Sea
United Shipbuilding Corporation
(Russia), 60
United States (U.S.)
    Arctic waters control by,
    80–84
    Canada Arctic territory claim
    and, 77
    Coast Guard, 82, 141
    Department of Interior, 116
    Energy Information Adminis-
    tration (EIA), 165, 166
    Fish and Wildlife Service
    (USFWS), 122

Geological Survey, 58, 117,
    160, 167
national security of, 137–142
National Snow and Ice Data
    Center, 115
Outer Continental Shelf
    (OCS), 139, 142, 162
position on Arctic territory,
    60–61
shipping lanes and, 81–83
transit fees, 84
trilateral agreement with,
    83–84
See also Oil drilling
Uranium resources, 160

V

von Geyer, Felix, 143–148

W

Walsh, Bryan, 87
Watt-Cloutier, Shelia, 93
West Antarctic Ice Sheet, 91
Wilson, Edward, 16
Wolfe, Adam, 56–62
Woodard, Colin, 89–93
Wordie ice shelf, 90
World Meteorological Organiza-
    tion, 37
World Park Antarctica (song),
    129–130
World Wildlife Fund (WWF), 125

Y

Young, Oran, 68